Girl Power!

A GIRL'S
DEVOTIONAL

Girl Power! A Girl's Devotional

Copyright 2021
ISBN: 978-0-9884572-3-2
reCreator - Mel Banks II
Cover and interior design: LTD², Larry Taylor, Designer
Cover and interior photos: iStock Photography
Originally compiled by Stephanie Perry Moore for Urban Spirit Publishing Co Editors
© Urban Spirit! Publishing and Media Company is an African American owned company based in Atlanta, GA. You can find more information at http://www.urbanspirit.biz/

Girl Power!

A GIRL'S DEVOTIONAL

With love for all the girls who use that magic to make their Daddy's and Mom's laugh, smile and frown with overwhelming love!

and to my favorite Kennedi D. T.

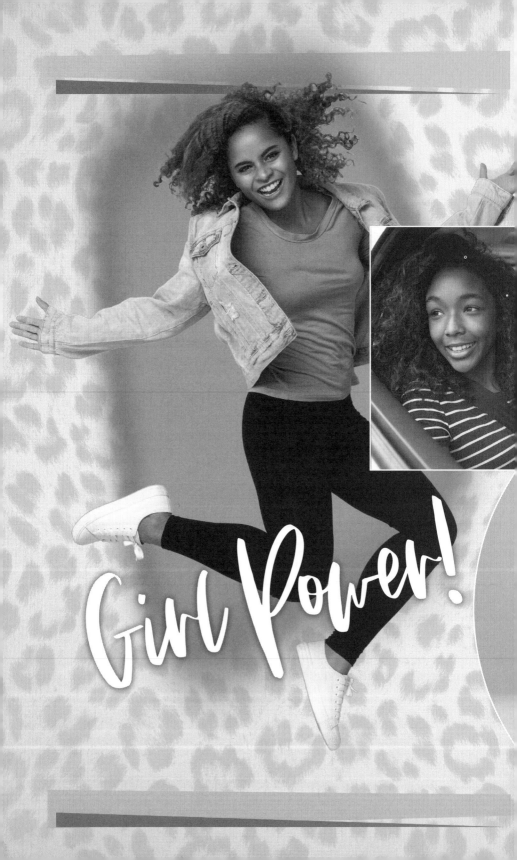

Girl Power!

THE TRUE MEANING OF CHRISTMAS

December

WEEK ONE: EXCELLENCE

Portia George

Day 1/Acts of Kindness

But as you excel in everything—in faith, in speech, in knowledge, and in all eagerness and in the love from us that is in you—make sure that you excel in this act of kindness too.

2 CORINTHIANS 8:7

A missionary from the United States was teaching in South Africa. During the Christmas season, one of his students, MoDue, noticed the sadness in his teacher's eyes. He asked his teacher what was troubling him. The teacher expressed his longing for a Christmas tree. It didn't have to be very big, but it would remind him of his family at home.

A few days passed and the teacher noticed that MoDue was absent. A full week passed, and as the teacher was placing things on the board in preparation of the day's lesson, he looked up and there was MoDue standing with a small treetop at his side.

He said, "Teacher, this is for you. I hope this will bring you the happiness and joy you bring us."

The teacher went to take Modue's hand and noticed the deep cuts and bruises on his feet, legs and hands. He said, "MoDue, what happened to you?"

"I had to go through several villages, climb trees, and cut this treetop with a sharp stone. But teacher, don't worry, God took good care of me. The walk is a part of my gift."

He gave the best he had, a walk of excellence and determination.

———————

Our lives as Christians should demonstrate to the world that we are followers and imitators of Christ. Excellence in our lives is defined as becoming more like Christ. "For ye were sometimes darkness, but now are ye light in the Lord: walk as children of light:...acceptable unto the Lord. And have no fellowship with the unfruitful works of darkness, but rather reprove them. For it is a shame even to speak of those things which are done of them in secret" (Ephesians 5:8 12).

APPLICATION

Are there any elderly or sick people you might do some shopping for, or who may need you to walk with them to the doctor's office or even the mailbox? Oh, how your act of kindness would lift their spirit.

PRAYER

Lord, lead as I walk in excellence each day for thee, striving to be the best I can be in my school, my church, and throughout my community. Help me to think of things that are excellent and pure in your sight. In Jesus' name, Amen.

DAY 2

EXCELLENCE IN KNOWLEDGE

For wisdom is a defense, and money is a defense: but the excellency of knowledge is, that wisdom giveth life to those who have it.

ECCLESIASTES 7:12

A few years ago, I made a conscious decision to carry gold dollars in my purse that I would give to kids of all ages whom I caught "doing good." Why? First, approximately 85% of gold comes from Africa. Second, I believe in rewarding others for a job well done, no matter how minimal the task might seem to others.

I remember one summer when I was visiting my sister. Her community was sponsoring a drill-team competition for the neighboring cities. One performer impressed me above all other contestants. It was a drummer, and he was not much bigger than the drum set he was carrying.

The whole team was dependent on his ability to keep the team in step. When the competition was over, unfortunately, the little drummer's team was not one of the winning teams. But the little fellow didn't seem too sad, for he knew in his heart that he had given his all. I began to work my way through the crowd to seek out the drummer so I could say thanks. When I approached him, I told him not to be concerned about the decision of the judges; he was the best drummer of all the teams. I then rewarded him with a gold dollar. I told him that it had the same significance as pinning a gold medal on him, given that he put forth a performance of excellence. He said, "Thank you!" He ran and told the captain of the team what I shared with him.

Gold was one of the priceless gifts given to baby Jesus by one of the wise men. Gold was a customary gift given to kings; how fitting that such a gift was given to baby Jesus. The countries from where these three wise men had traveled viewed items such as gold with high regard.

APPLICATION

Encourage someone for a job well done, no matter how small the task. Look for ways to let others know that they're appreciated with golden words, "Good job, way to go."

PRAYER

Lord, help me to stay in step with the beating of your drum, stay in tune with the steps you have in my life. As I read your Word daily, impart to me the excellence of knowledge so that I may impart life to others through your Word. Amen.

DAY 3
EXCELLENCE IN POWER

But we have this treasure in earthen vessels, that the excellency of the power may be of God, and not of us.

2 CORINTHIANS 4:7

Julie was diagnosed with juvenile diabetes when she was 8. After that, she did all the right things: proper diet, exercise, checking her insulin, and regular visits to the doctor. Despite all that, Julie's foot had to be amputated during her sophomore year in high school. Now she was really mad with God.

First, he allowed me to have the disease, she fumed to herself, *and now, after I do everything to take care of myself, He allowed them to take my foot.* She had forgiven God, sort of, at the time of the diagnosis but this time, no way. She thought, *I don't deserve this.*

———

We keep missing the fact that we are not in control, God is. Whatever God has for us is an excellent mission. No matter what our physical circumstances or appearance, God did not make a mistake with us and we are still awesome and fearfully made. Thank God for who you are and thrive in all that He has given you. Above all else, gain knowledge from Him about why you are who you are. You'll find that there is no one on this earth better suited than you for the task God has for you.

APPLICATION

Allow God to use you. Visit a neighborhood nursing home or hospital, share your sweetness with a smile, prayer, card, or a song. Express the story about the gifts Jesus received as a baby.

PRAYER

Lord, thank you for the treasures we each posses and for the knowledge of the gifts you received as a little baby. Help me to apply this wisdom when I select gifts for my family and friends. Thank you for the greatest gift of all, your Son, Jesus. Amen

DAY 4
MORAL EXCELLENCE

*According as his divine power hath given unto us all things that
pertain unto life and godliness, through the knowledge of him
that hath called us to glory and virtue.*

2 PETER 1:3

In Old Testament times, shepherding was an honorable occupation. But by the first century, the economy had changed, and shepherding was no longer attractive. Shepherds were not the kind of people one would think should be around a newborn child.

Angels coming to lowly shepherds in a field was an incredible expression of heavenly splendor. These shepherds were special; they were the first to hear about the Savior's birth. These shepherds were doing a superb job, not recognized by man, honored by God himself. God called them with his own glory to proclaim the birth of the Savior. They went with haste to the infant.

They found the baby Jesus lying in a manger, surrounded by animals. The shepherd made known what the prophets told concerning this child. They returned to their field, glorifying and praising God.

———

God is not a respecter of persons. That means that what he does for me, he'll do for you. Circumstances may be different; some may be born into more difficult circumstances than another's, but each of us can follow the moral high road, wherever God has placed us. Even more, we can all do the work that God has called us to do, within the circumstances where God has placed us. Even when we get off track and into sin, God will take us and use us in our repentance. Yes, God is good all the time.

APPLICATION

List all the characteristics of your life that the world would find undesirable. Then list all the ways that God has used you or those characteristics to bless you and others.

PRAYER

Lord, we thank you for the example using ordinary people, people whom we least expect to do your work. Thank you for your baby Son, who accomplished the greatest task of all time. May we recognize your power daily and give you praise each day for the knowledge of your Word. Amen.

DAY 5
EXCELLENCE, A PRICELESS GIFT

And now, my daughter, fear not; I will do to thee thou requirest: for all of the city of my people doth know that thou art a virtuous woman.

RUTH 3:11

Mary had been traveling on a donkey, worn and weary. She gave birth in a stable and laid her baby in a lowly manger. Shepherds came from watching their fields. Wise men, following the star in the set, came from the East to bring gifts to this new little king: Jesus, the priceless gift.

The three wise men represent three things: God is present in the word, if only we follow the star. Each of us has a gift to bring to the Savior. Finally, the journey always leads to Jesus, even if we do not know where we are now going.

The first wise men brought gold, a symbol that Jesus is king. The second brought frankincense, a symbol that Jesus is God. The third bought myrrh, the spice of wisdom and of death, a symbol that Jesus is the true wisdom who has come into this world and that, through his death, we shall be redeemed.

Being a mother is one of the greatest gifts a woman of God can be given. Not every woman is called to be a mother, but if God blesses you to give birth to a child one

day, nurture and bring that child up in the fear and admonition of the Lord. Watch your child grow to be his or her own person in the Lord; there's no greater reward.

Becoming whatever God called you to be is a demonstration of excellence. It cannot be purchased. It is something that you must attain.

APPLICATION

As you look forward the new year, set your standards high. Ask God to direct your path, to help you succeed in all you do at home, school, church, and work.

PRAYER

Father, help me to make the right choices in all that I do. Let others see excellence in my walk and my talk. Help me to affirm others as they do their best. Thank you for a brand new year. Amen.

THE TRUE MEANING OF CHRISTMAS

December

WEEK TWO: VALUES

Michele Clark Jenkins

Day 1 / Living Life in Peace or Pieces

For they that are after flesh do mind the things of the flesh: but they that are after the Spirit the things of the Spirit. For to be carnally minded is death; but to be spiritually minded is life and peace.

ROMANS 8:5,6

At 14, Carolyn was already experimenting with boys. Her parents were aware of what was going on and tried to cut her off from the "bad influences." Problem was, Carolyn was her own bad influence. In her mind, anything she felt like doing, anytime she felt like doing it, was okay. No boundaries. She quickly found out that no matter what her parents did, they couldn't lock her up for 24 hours a day.

At 16, Carolyn had already been pregnant twice. But that was okay with her; abortions were just more expensive birth control. She actually did pretty well in school and

always stopped short of really crossing the law, or at least getting caught. She'd already tried smoking and drinking. She didn't like cigarettes much but loved to drink beer. She was queen of her own kingdom. She ruled her own world.

Without boundaries we are just out there in chaos. God created the Garden of Eden as a special place for Adam and Eve. But there were some boundaries. God told Adam that he could eat the fruit from any tree, but he could not eat fruit from the tree that gave knowledge of good and evil, otherwise he would die. Adam and Eve listened to the lies of the Devil, disobeyed God's rule, and ate the forbidden fruit. It was the first sin and it was a big one, so big that we've received an enormous inheritance from them—the sin nature.

Without any controls, we would just do any old thing, simply because we felt like it. That's why we have parents. Our parents have to protect us from ourselves. Do you know what would happen if your parents went away for a week and left you at home with money, the keys to the car, maybe a full liquor cabinet, and no rules? Your parents would hope that you would live by whatever values they had already taught you. But those values can get mixed up with other things, such as what your friends think. The world is made up of a lot of people who do what their flesh tells them to do. That's the very opposite of what God would have you to do.

APPLICATION

Think about what you would do differently in your life if your parents weren't around. Do you think that without parental supervision you'd be living your life God's way?

PRAYER

Lord, I see that I am imperfect and that my flesh tugs on me every day to do only what feels good. But, Lord, I am trusting the Holy Spirit to show me a better way, a way that will please you. Amen.

DAY 2
WHAT THE WORLD SAYS IS COOL

Beware lest any man spoil you through philosophy and vain deceit,
after the tradition of men, after the rudiments of the world,
and not after Christ.

COLOSSIANS 2:8

Ceci was up on all the latest fashions and trends. She was the one everyone looked to for the latest fashion trends. Her parents could afford to buy her the newest designer clothes, so she rearely wore an outfit more than twice during the school year.

Ceci was not just outer fluff, she was very smart and very political. She knew all the social and political issues of the day in the same way that she watched the fashion designers, week to week. It really depended on what her favorite actor, singer, or peer group thought. Ceci was no dummy. This made her always politically correct and popular. Ceci believed in God and that the Bible was mostly true, but she thought that some of it was just plain old-fashioned and outdated.

APPLICATION

Get a one year Bible and start to read it everyday. Write down things that you really don't agree with. Then pray over them and ask the Lord to shine light into those dark places for you and write them on your heart.

PRAYER

Lord, I don't want to be a slave to the newest trend, like my ancestors were slaves to a physical master. Lord, let me have the freedom of knowing the Holy Spirit and letting the Holy Spirit be the trendsetter in my life. Amen.

DAY 3

MORE THAN JUST FOLLOWING THE RULES

Therefore by the deeds of the law there shall no flesh be justified in his sight: for by the law is the knowledge of sin.

ROMANS 3:20

For a while, Jody was very active in her youth group. She remembered the Ten Commandments from Sunday school and lived by them. When she read the Bible, she made lists of all the things it said she was supposed to do and all the things she wasn't supposed to do, and she put them up on her bulletin board. There were a lot of do's and don'ts. She even stopped eating pork and shellfish after reading the book of Leviticus. However, there wasn't much satisfaction for her in any of this. She began to see it as just another set of rules she had to remember. She soon left the youth group, disappointed that God didn't seem any different from her parents or teachers. *He just wants me to follow a bunch of silly rules*, she thought.

Rules have nothing to do with our relationship with God. What He wants from us, and has always wanted from us, even in the days of the law, is for us to have faith in him. God gave laws to show them that, just like with Adam and Eve, they would not be able to keep them. It's not just you, none of us are perfect and do everything

right. "For all have sinned, and come short of the glory of God" (Romans 3:23). People are sinners. The law showed us that we could not do it on our own and how much we need a savior.

APPLICATION

Think back over the last 24 hours. How many times have you "broken the rules"? Remember to include all the bad thoughts you had because those are sins too.

PRAYER

Father, I love you and I want to walk in your ways. I know that when I have faith in you and use your Word, not as a rule book but as a book of power and authority, I will see and feel all that you have for me. Amen.

DAY 4

GOOD PEOPLE—BAD PEOPLE

For by grace are ye saved through faith; and that not of yourselves:
it is the gift of God: not of works, lest any man should boast.

EPHESIANS 2:8,9

Tiffany knew that she was going to heaven. She was a good person who did lots of good things for many people. She volunteered at the local nursing home every Saturday. She went to the veterans hospital at Christmastime every year to take cookies to the patients there. She was responsible for helping raise almost $1,000 for homeless children in foreign nations. She also got her parents to investigate being foster parents, and it looked as if that was going to happen soon. She knew that she had earned a place in heaven.

———————

You don't get into heaven because you are a good person. You get into heaven because you received the free gift of salvation by receiving Jesus Christ as your Lord and Savior. If we could earn salvation, Jesus would never have had to die on the cross for us. To think that we can somehow earn a place in heaven is to make the cross and Jesus meaningless. Jesus paid the price for our sin.

APPLICATION

If you have been thinking that you can save yourself by your good works, pray now to receive Christ as your Lord and Savior. Confess that you are a sinner and ask Jesus to come into your heart right now.

PRAYER

Lord, I have sinned and fallen short of your glory. Forgive me all of my sins and wash me clean. You have already paid the price for my sins and I worship you and praise your name for saving me. Please Lord, come into my heart now. I believe in you as my Lord and Savior. Amen.

DAY 5
BY THE WORD AND SPIRIT

For ye were sometimes darkness, but now are ye light in the Lord: walk as children of light: (for the fruit of the Spirit is in all goodness and righteousness and truth;) proving what is acceptable unto the Lord.

EPHESIANS 5:8-10

Abi loved the Lord with all her heart. Although she was only 13, she had known the Lord since she was 8. At first, she had very little learned knowledge of who he is. She just grew to know his voice when he spoke to her spirit and began to read and understand the Word of God. God revealed things to her as she read it and meditated on it.

She didn't really think about following any rules, but she would wake up in the morning and start talking to the Lord immediately. She asked him about her day, praised him, and asked him some hard questions about what he intended for her to do and what he really wanted for us all. Usually, she would feel directed to a certain verse to read that day, or it would be weird that the next verse she read was about the very thing she was talking to God about. Throughout the day, it seemed as if everything and everybody around her worked to confirm what God had already told her.

God is the source of all the values we should be living in our lives. He is the first and the last say in it all. So it all starts by finding out what will please him. God has

given us many answers to that question in his Word, found in the Bible, and he tells us to seek him and his kingdom (Matthew 6: 33) and to get his wisdom (Proverbs 4: 7, 8). God doesn't change and neither do his values for Christian living. But the Lord has made it so easy for us to know which way to go. He left us with the Holy Spirit to lead us and guide us in his ways.

APPLICATION

Read Ephesians 6 and pray through the process of putting on the armor of God. Then imagine putting on each piece of the armor.

PRAYER

Lord, I live by faith in you. I will be strong in you and the power of your might. I will put on your armor so that I will be able to stand against the wiles of the Devil and live a life according to the values that you have laid on my heart. I thank you and praise you, Lord. Amen.

THE TRUE MEANING OF CHRISTMAS

December

Rachelle Hollie Guillory

Day 1 / The Promised Gift—the Holy Spirit

*Then Peter said unto them, Repent and be baptized every one of you
in the name of Jesus Christ for the remission of sins,
and ye shall receive the gift of the Holy Ghost.*

ACTS 2:38

Ever since she was a toddler, Ernestine went to church every Sunday with her parents. But when she reached 16, she felt a void and thought there had to be something more to church than listening to the choir and the sermon each week. Britni, Ernestine's friend, asked if she had received Christ and the gift of the Holy Spirit since she believed. "No," Ernestine responded.

"Salvation is a gift; it's free," Britni told her. "All you need to do is believe what the scriptures say and receive Christ. His spirit is promised to you.

There is no greater gift to receive than the gift of salvation. When you receive salvation you receive God's Spirit, the Holy Spirit. The Holy Ghost is comforter, guide, and sustainer to those counted among the body of Christ. When we do not know what or how to pray, the Holy Spirit will speak spiritually for us in ways that our natural mouths could never utter. We need God's Spirit in order to successfully walk in the daily Christian walk.

APPLICATION

Today, share the good news of God's gift with someone. Tell the person that she, too, can be a recipient of the most precious gift God ever offered to mankind—Jesus Christ. If you have not received this promised treasure, search the Scriptures and discover how you can receive Jesus Christ and the Holy Ghost.

PRAYER

Father, I recognize that I need your Spirit to help me live the Christian life. Help me, Father to share the good news about this precious gift of salvation with others. In your name, I pray. Amen.

DAY 2
WHICH GIFT IS FOR ME?

*But covet earnestly the best gifts:
and yet shew I unto you a more excellent way.*

1 CORINTHIANS 12:31

Kamryn's parents were bubbling with Joy. It was their daughters third Christmas, and they thought it would be her most memorable because she would have a better understanding of opening gifts. There were more than 20 gifts for Kamryn under the tree, each varying in size and wrapping.

Charles, her big brother, decided he would assist his sister. "Open the big one, the big one," he yelled as he jumped up and down and handed the big package to his sister. "No," Kamryn said as he dropped the gift.
"Here, Kamryn," her mother urged, "open this one, I think this is the one you'll like the most."
"No," Kamryn responded again. Never losing focus, little Kamryn kneeled and picked up the most awkwardly shaped gift. It was smaller than the other ones and was wrapped in plain, brown-bag paper. Little Kamryn was drawn to that gift.

———————

God is the giver of all gifts. No one can give anyone else a spiritual gift. It is up to the individual to discern what gift God gave them before the foundation of the world. Search your heart for that particular "thing" that compels your spirit and which you

are passionate about. Take a spiritual gifts test or inventory at your church. Ask God to reveal to you what that special gift he chose especially for you.

APPLICATION

Today, take the time to examine your spiritual gifts. Ask God to guide you as to what avenues you should take in order to use your gifts in ways in which he would be pleased. Remember, it is important to nurture your gifts with study and application.

PRAYER

Lord, I recognize that you endowed me with spiritual gifts before I was even conceived. Open my eyes and divinely reveal my gift to me so that I can use them to your glory and honor. In the name of Jesus, I pray. Amen.

DAY 3
WRITING YOUR GIFT LIST

If ye then, being evil, know how to give good gifts to your children,
how much more shall your Father which is in heaven
give good things to them that ask him?

MATTHEW 7:11

Ariel sat at her desk writing a Christmas list for her parents. Since she had been a little girl, Ariel's parents had told her how the tradition of Santa Claus had begun. She know from whom the gifts under her tree came. Now, 9 years old and an only child, Ariel had already been the recipient of almost any tangible gift a girl could wish to have.

Suddenly, she stopped writing and began to cry. She knew there was one gift that her parents could not give her. Ariel's mother asked her why she was crying.

"Because I really want a special gift for Christmas, and I know you and Dad can't get it for me," she told her mother. "I want Grandmother to be healed of the cancer that's making her so sick," Ariel cried.
"I see," her mother said. "Well then instead of wiring a list for Santa, address your letter, "Dear Savior…"

If they could, most parents wold give their child every good thing that they could acquire. It is the desire of loving parents to protect, direct, and indulge their children.

Today's Scripture plainly answers that God our Father, who is incapable of wickedness, can give us so much more than we could ever imagine giving our children.

APPLICATION

Write a spiritual gift list today! Read Romans 12: 6-11 and study the gifts of the Spirit. Ask God to work through you and bestow upon you one of those gifts. God will reveal the gift that he has chosen for you in due time.

PRAYER

Jesus, I have a special desire for a specific spiritual gift, but I want to do your will. Reveal to me that special spiritual gift or gifts that you designed personally for me. In the name of Jesus, I pray. Amen.

Day 4
YOU CAN'T PAY FOR IT!

For the gifts and calling of God are without repentance.

ROMANS 11:29

Julia was a new convert to Christianity. As she sat in the congregation every Sunday, she noticed the working of many gifts in the lives of many of the other congregants. A seasoned saint, Sister Benita, noticed that Julia's heart seemed heavy.

"Baby sis," Sister Benita asked, "what's on your mind?"

Julia responded, "Everyone here seems to have a spiritual gift from the Lord. I'd like to be used by God, but I've done too many terrible things in my life for God to allow me to have one of these spiritual gifts."

"Everyone has sinned, baby" Sister Benita told Julia. "God doesn't give us these gifts based on merit. There is absolutely nothing anyone could do that would make them deserving of God's gift's, love, mercy, or grace. You have your gift already. God gave it to you before your were born. Believe that!"

The gifts of God and his calling are priceless. Before the foundation of the world— before you were conceived—God knew which gifts he would bestow upon you. There are times when the enemy would have you to believe that because of your iniquities

or because of your past, you are unworthy to have or use spiritual gifts. But God can use a sinner to bless others if he wants to do so. There is no amount of money you could find that can pay God for one of his gifts. His gifts are priceless, precious, and invaluable.

APPLICATION

Today, do not allow the devil to trick you into thinking that you are unworthy of any gift from God. Remember, God's gifts were given to you before you took you first breath. When you are battling with your worthiness as it relates to the use of the gift God has given you, speak the Word of God to the devil and let him know that "the gifts and calling of God are without repentance."

PRAYER

Jesus, I thank you for the gifts you have given me. Please help me to use them wisely and to recognize that you gave them to me undeservingly. Help me to remember that the gifts I have are for your good pleasure. In the name of Jesus, I pray. Amen.

DAY 5
CHRISTIAN FRUIT CAKE

But the fruit of the Spirit is love, joy, peace, longsuffering, gentleness, goodness, faith, meekness, temperance: against such there is no law.

GALATIANS 5:22,23

The Christmas season was in full effect. But Charity was not in the holiday spirit. She was quite annoyed with the hustle and bustle, and quite frankly, the crowds irritated her. Her friends, Dale and Joseph, met her at church. They each volunteered to assist in the distribution of holiday baskets for the needy in the surrounding neighborhoods.

Charity became noticeably agitated with the neighborhood based recipients. She was impatient, she argued with them, her face communicated unhappiness, and she refused to listen to anything the people tried to say to her.

Dale pulled his friend to the side and told her that he knew what she could give each of the people in the line as a gift from her for Christmas. Irritated that he pulled her away, she asked sarcastically, "And what might that be?"

"Give me the gift of displaying the fruit of the Spirit as you communicate with them. You'll feel better, and I guarantee you that they will be happy."

The spirit of Christmas truly is illustrative of the fruit of the Spirit. Although the existence and working of the fruit of the Spirit should shine in your life throughout the year, its display can be especially helpful during the time of year when the suicide rate in typically high. People who have lost a family member or someone close to them become particularly depressed during the holidays. As a young woman of God, your spirit should demonstrate the fruit of the Spirit. Instead of giving a natural fruit cake to your friends and family, give them spiritual fruit.

APPLICATION

Make a spiritual fruit cake out of your life and give it as a gift to those you associate with. Take a bowl of love, a dash of joy, a sprinkle of peace, a teaspoon of long-suffering, a chunk of gentleness, a tablespoon of goodness, a cup of faith, an ounce of meekness, and a load of temperance. Mix them together in your spirit. Then let it rise.

PRAYER

Jesus, I thank you for the fruit of the Spirit. Help me to incorporate its components in my daily life and deliberations with others. In the name of Jesus, I pray. Amen.

THE TRUE MEANING OF CHRISTMAS

December

WEEK FOUR: CHRISTMAS

Sabrina Black

Day 1 / Another Angel with Good News

And the angel answering said unto him, I am Gabriel, that stand in the presence of God; and am sent to speak unto thee, and to shew you thee these glad tidings.... And the angel came in unto her, and said, Hail, thou that art highly favored, the Lord is with thee: blessed art thou among women.

LUKE 1:19,28

Gabrielle always loved her name. Her parents referred to her as their little angel who would bring good news. She knew that she was named after the angel Gabriel in the book of Luke. Most of her friends talked in the month of December about the Christmas story, the birth of Jesus Christ. But Gabrielle talked about it all year round, especially when someone commented about her name. She was excited about what God had revealed to her regarding her purpose in life.

The news that she shared with others was simple: "For nothing is impossible with God." When Gabrielle shared the Christmas story, she told it from a different angle.

She talked about how God had allowed an old barren woman (Elizabeth) and then a virgin (Mary) to be pregnant. If he could do that, he could do anything.

———————

Gabrielle is blessed to be named after an angel, but no matter what your name may be, God has a purpose for your life. What is the good news that you are able to share with others regarding the birth of Christ?

APPLICATION

Make a list today of five people who need to hear the purpose for which Jesus was born. Then tell them that nothing is impossible with God, which means he can do everything. What do you need God to do in your life?

PRAYER

Oh, Lord, I want to tell others about you all year round, not just at Christmas. Give me a story to tell—people need to know that nothing is impossible with God. Amen.

DAY 2

THE TRADITION OF THE WORD

In the beginning was the Word, and the Word was with God,
and the Word was God.... And the Word was made flesh,
and dwelt among us, (and we beheld his glory,
the glory as of the only begotten of the Father,)
full of grace and truth.

JOHN 1: 1,14

Shantel was glad to meet Andre, a nice Christian guy whom her family liked. They approved of her spending time with him. This would be her first Christmas Eve away from home and the latest in the evening that Shantel had ever been allowed to stay out. Andre's family celebrated Christmas at midnight on the 24th of December. As part of their tradition, they would pass the big family Bible around to each person there and have them read a few verses and share how God had blessed them throughout the year. Shantel was so moved by the time of sharing around the Word of God. She sensed the presence of God in the room and felt an inner peace when Andre read from John 1. This was a holiday tradition that she would always remember.

Most families have a holiday tradition. What does your family do to celebrate Christmas, the birth of Christ? Family traditions may include exchanging gifts, big feasts of food, and visits from out-of-town relatives. But does your tradition include the presence of God, the reading of his Word, and the recounting of blessings?

APPLICATION

Consider starting a new tradition with your family this Christmas. Make a list of three Bible verses that really have a significant meaning for you and share these with your family members. Encourage them to share their favorite verses with you and tell how God has blessed them throughout the year.

PRAYER

Oh, God, thank you for becoming flesh and dwelling among us. Thank you that you, through your Holy Spirit, are still, "God with us." I am so blessed by your presence and your Word. I want others to be blessed, too. Amen.

DAY 3

NOW THAT YOU ARE FOUND —STILL SEEK HIM

For the Son of man is come to seek and to save that which is lost.

LUKE 19:10

"Wise men still seek him," the postcard had read, but she couldn't find it anywhere. She wanted to share this card with some friends and encourage them to seek God through studying the Word. It seemed that Samatra was always seeking, searching and looking for something. And as much as she hated to admit it, her mother knew that it was mostly because she didn't look very hard for things. Her mom, of course, could come into her room, wade through a sea of crumpled papers or misplaced clothing, and find the "lost" item in the most unlikely place.

The prophecy was that the Savior would be born in the City of David. Bethlehem was not the sort of place that you'd look for a King. However, Luke 2:4 reveals that, in this most unlikely place, Christ was born.

Samatra would have missed the Savior because she doesn't look hard enough for anything and often gives up without exploring all the possibilities. Samatra was

relieved that Jesus sought her and that she responded to the gospel when she was 7. Now she seeks him daily as she studies the Word. If she can't find anything else she knows where to find God.

Thank God that Jesus came to seek those who are lost. Thank God that he found Samatra and that he found you. On a small piece of paper, write two things. On one side, write one of the focus Scriptures for today and share your personal testimony about when the Lord found you and saved you. On the back write: "Wise Men/Women still seek him; look harder." Keep this in your wallet, purse, or backpack as a reminder.

APPLICATION

Look into the Word every day and ask God to show you something new. Look to different parts of the Bible; it may seem unlikely that God will speak to you through books that are unfamiliar, but look harder.

PRAYER

Oh Lord, you are always here. Help me to be wise and spend time with you daily and not somehow overlook you. Open my eyes so that I may seek you, find you, and worship you. Amen.

DAY 4
HUMBLE ACCEPTANCE

And Mary said, Behold the handmaid of the Lord;
be it unto me according to thy word.

LUKE 1:38

"This can't be. I'm not even running for office! Are they sure that they don't want someone else to do this?" Michelle whispered to Renee as she reluctantly accepted the nomination for presidency.

"Sure, there are others, but you are the one we want to represent us. You have the right spirit, the right attitude, and the right heart."

Renee was a great source of encouragement. Michelle knew that being president was more than having a title; it was about serving others. The nomination came as quite a surprise. Although there were other students who really wanted the responsibility of leadership, Michelle was content without having a role in the student government. Now that she had accepted, she would trust God to help her in this just as he had helped her in everything else.

God is often looking for someone lowly and meek to fulfill his plan. He doesn't always select people who are font and center and shouting, "Pick me, pick me!" God knows your character and who he can trust with various assignments. God has a plan for your life, but you have to accept his will. Think for a minute about the one thing that you know that you should be doing, but are refusing to do. You may even be saying, "This can't be." Mary accepted God's will and so did Michelle. Will you?

APPLICATION

Write on a sheet of paper what you believe God is calling you to do. Then say it aloud and pray. "Be it unto me according to thy Word."

PRAYER

Oh Lord, help me to put my life in your hands and to keep your will first in my life. I want to follow your plans, but I'm not sure what they are. Speak, Lord; your servant is listening. Make it plain and help me to humble myself to accept your will for me. Amen.

DAY 5
THE GREATEST GIFT OF ALL —TO KNOW HIM

That the God of our Lord Jesus Christ, the Father of glory,
may give unto you the spirit of wisdom and revelation
in the knowledge of him.

EPHESIANS 1:17

They were all very excited about the upcoming weekend. Roneshia, Shelly, and Gwenevere had been exchanging Christmas gifts since they were in the eighth grade. Part of the excitement was discussing what had been the best gift to date. This year, Gwenevere wanted to give what she knew would be the greatest gift of all. She remembered when Roneshia was baptized but realized that she needed to know God better, and she wasn't really sure about Shelly. Beyond just going to church and participating in the youth events, Shelly really did not have a relationship with Christ. Gwenevere prayed daily regarding the gifts she wanted to give as the weekend approached. This would be a special time.

"Do you know that you know the Lord Jesus Christ?" Before they could answer, she explained that her desire for them (no matter what their response) was that they would know him better. "Who is Jesus to you? Some say that he is a good person, great humanitarian, great philanthropist, or great prophet. Others say the Son of God, the Savior of the world. Mary's baby boy, the one who died on the cross."

With tears in her eyes, Gwenevere said, "You two are my best friends, and it's important to me that you have the greatest gift of all—that you *know* him and not just *about* him."

People who really know him talk differently about him. They give a personal, intimate response in answer to the question, "Do you know him?" Their responses may include: Jesus is the lover of my soul, my deliverer, my Savior, my friend. When we talk about knowing the Lord Jesus Christ, we are talking about a mutual friendship, one where we know each other. The greatest gift you can give is the knowledge of who Christ is and wants to be in the life of your friends.

APPLICATION

If you really want to know Jesus, study the book of John. In that text, Jesus himself tells you who he is. Before reading the text, make a list of all the names by which you may know Jesus. Then see how many of them are found in John. Studying the Word is a great way to get to know him better.

PRAYER

Oh, Lord, thank you for giving me the greatest gift of all—your Son, my Savior, Jesus Christ. Thank you that I am able to share this gift with others, knowing that it is the greatest gift anyone could ever receive. Lord, help me to know you better. Amen.

GETTING THE BEST START POSSIBLE

January

WEEK ONE: POSITIVE THINKING

Jennifer Keitt

DAY 1 / Thinking My Way to a Brand-New Life

And be not conformed to the world: but be ye transformed by the renewing of your mind, that ye may prove what is that good, and acceptable, and perfect, will of God.

R O M A N S 1 2 : 2

"I just don't think I can do it," Lisa moaned to her friend, Kelley.
"Sure you can, girl, just practice these moves with me."
"Kelley, you're always so sure and positive about things. Why is that?" Lisa questioned.
"Well, my mom always told me that we can do anything that we think we can do, so I think I can do it all, girl!"
"Wow," Lisa said, "I always think I can't do anything..."

———————

There is a brand-new life waiting for you right between your ears! Researchers say that we think, on average, 50,000 thoughts a day. That's more than one thought per second. If you're spending time thinking negatively, you're going to have a rotten, negative life. But if you start thinking about God's positive ways and the great things that he has for you, you can have a better life. You'll have all that God wants for you!

God tells us plainly how to change. "And be not conformed to this world: but be ye transformed by the renewing of your mind" (Romans 12: 2). Change comes when you make the decision to consciously change how you're thinking. Do you always imagine the worst? Are you always struggling with not feeling that you're good enough, strong enough, cute enough, or popular enough? Then check your thinking. Whatever you're thinking in your heart, that's what you are or will become. God wants you to be an awesome woman. You can be, if you think and believe that you can!

APPLICATION

Here's what you need to do to start your new life. Make a concerted effort to put at least one of the steps into action today:

Decide that you want to change for the right reasons—to please God. Begin with deciding to change to become the young woman God wants you to be.

Understand that change always takes time so don't be in a hurry. Be consistent in reading passages in the Bible about how God created you. Don't worry if it doesn't seem as though things are changing in a day or a few weeks. Just know that God is doing work in you.

Use the Bible as your main resource for changing your thinking. The Bible says "This book of the law shall not depart out of thy mouth; but thou shalt meditate therein: ...for then thou shalt make thy way prosperous, and then thou shalt have good success" (Joshua 1: 8). That's what you want. A new life that is successful!

You are on your way to a brand-new you with brand-new godly thinking!

PRAYER

Father, help me to think like you! I want to think your thoughts. Help me to change my outlook. I want more of what you want for me. Help me to think positive thoughts and to view my life the way you view it. Thank you, Father. In Jesus' name, Amen!

DAY 2

BRAIN FOOD—WATCH WHAT YOU'RE EATING!

Keep thy heart with all diligence; for out of it are the issues of life.

PROVERBS 4:23

"I listened to my new album all night last night." Jill exclaimed. "I love his new 'get you in the mood' love song," she told her sister, Brenda.

"Jill, I don't know how you listen to that stuff all day and night. You never take your headphones off!"

"What's the big deal? I'm not hurting anybody!"

"Well," Brenda said, "you are hurting somebody—YOU! The more you listen to that stuff, the more you're going to think about it."

"So what?" Jill shot back angrily.

"So, what you think, you become!

Everyday, we flood our hearts and minds with all kinds of information. We listen to our friends, our families, our teachers, TV, radio, movies, and books. We are overloaded with information.

As a young woman, it's important that you watch your "diet". The diet that I'm talking about, though, isn't the food you put into your mouth. Its what you put into your mind. The Bible encourages you to be very careful about what you think. You've

heard the saying, "You are what you eat." Well, how true it is. What you listen to on an ongoing basis automatically begins to feed your mind and that, in turn, fuels your thoughts. The Bible makes it clear that what you think could ruin your life.

You want a great life. Well, the key to getting this great life is to begin now by thinking great thoughts. The way you think great thoughts is to carefully select a "mental diet" that is rich in positive, kind, wonderful things.

APPLICATION

Take today to begin training yourself to eat a better mental diet. The Bible encourages us: "Finally brethren, whatsoever things are true, whatsoever things are honest, whatsoever things are just, whatsoever things are pure, whatsoever things are lovely, whatsoever things are of good report; if there be any virtue, and if there be any praise, think on these things." (Philippians 4: 8). Our exercise for today is simple. Turn off the TV, radio, and your music. Get a piece of paper or a journal and a pencil or pen and find a quiet spot. Write down your good thoughts. Think about positive things in your life or about God and yourself for at least 5 minutes. Practice doing this at least twice a day. You will begin to find more positive thoughts filtering through your mind and allowing God to change your life one day at a time.

PRAYER

Father, help me to have a better mental diet. Help me to shut down all of the information being thrown at me every day. Help me to concentrate and develop good thoughts that will help my life grow better. Thank you for loving me enough to help me. In Jesus' name, I pray. Amen.

DAY 3
FORGETTING THOSE THINGS THAT ARE BEHIND

Brethren, I count not myself to have apprehended: but this one thing I do, forgetting those things which are behind, and reaching forth unto those things which are before, I press toward the mark for the prize of the high calling of God in Christ Jesus.

PHILIPPIANS 3:13,14

"For so long I thought I couldn't get an A in math," Lynn confided in her friend Derrick.
"Yeah, math has always been difficult for me too," Derrick commented.
"But, you know, Derrick, after I started really believing what my Sunday school teacher said—that we can do all things through Christ—things started turning around. I mean, I really believed I could get an A and I got it!
"Like magic?" Derrick questioned.
"No I had to first convince myself that I could do it. Then I sat down with my teacher and put together a plan. I studied like crazy. I even got a tutor, and it paid off in the end."

———

Old beliefs can have a devastating effect on our lives. What we've been thinking about since we were little can be the death of us when we start to grow up. If younger you thought you couldn't be a good student, or if you thought you weren't

pretty enough or athletic enough, you've probably run up against some serious limitations. You may have even begun to realize that those old ways of thinking have really boxed you in.

The Bible talks about this: "Don't look back." Your past—good and bad—should be used for historical reference only because it is no indication of what your future holds for you. Use your past just as you use encyclopedias: to find out how things were in the past. But rejoice, because Christ has so much more planned for your future, if he can just get you to break free from the bondage of old thoughts.

Breaking free will take a little work. When you try to break old ways of thinking, sometimes you have to really fight to forget. Think about this just as you wold a real fight. You must win; your life depends depends on it. You must take every negative old way of thinking under control and begin to redirect your thought life.

APPLICATION

Start to take stock of the old, negative thoughts that run through your mind throughout the day. You know, the ones that say how bad you were or how unpopular you feel. Every time an old, negative thought comes up, take it captive. That means to get it under the control of the Word of God. Don't let negative thoughts run freely in your brain. Stop them, check them against the the Word of God, and remove them from your thinking. You will soon find yourself victorious if you begin a lifestyle of doing this when those negative thoughts try to rise up.

PRAYER

Lord, I need to bring my old thoughts captive and replace them with new ways of thinking. Help me to forget the bad things of my past. Help me to forget the negative things about myself. Please cleanse my thoughts, make them pure, and help me to be a better thinker. In Jesus' name. Amen.

DAY 4

THINK AS GOD THINKS!

Set your affection on things above, not on things on the earth.

COLOSSIANS 3:2

Joan and Brenda were walking home from school one day, reflecting on life and other such issues. "I am so stressed out," Brenda confided.

"About what?" Joan asked.

"My mom and dad are at it again. I can't get any peace in that house, my report is due tomorrow, and I have cheerleading practice three days this week. I'm freaking out!"

"Girl, you've got to get control! Think about this. In heaven, there's no freaking out! God is always in control."

That's a cool thought," Brenda sighed. "I wish my life could be heavenly."

"It can," Joan encouraged. "Just think as God thinks!"

Forcing yourself to think as God thinks can be a very difficult thing to do sometimes. This is especially true when you are overloaded. The pressures of school, family troubles, friends—just life—sometimes can be overwhelming in your mind. You don't have to stay in the middle of all that mess and pressure. Think from a heavenly perspective.

I believe that's why God asked us to set our minds on things that are above, where Christ is. Setting our minds is an interesting concept. Imagine a TV set. Then see yourself flicking the remote to your favorite channel. That TV is tuned to that one

channel, and it won't move until you change it or turn off the TV. Well, it's the same with our minds. We have the capability to set our minds to one thought. We can think about the things that Christ is thinking about. We can take our minds off the things going on around us that are bad or overwhelming, and we can choose to think about godly things, heavenly things, and things that can bring us peace.

APPLICATION

Begin practicing tuning in and changing your "mind channel" throughout the day. When thoughts begin to come into your mind, imagine that you have a remote control. As the unwanted thoughts start to filter in, simply continue to change mind channels until you get to a thought that is from above. Keep changing the thoughts until you are thinking something good, true, and godly.

PRAYER

Lord, help me to keep my mind focused and set on the things that are where you are. Help me to have the mind of Christ in all things. Help me to develop a disciplined mind that is stayed on you. In Jesus' name. Amen!

DAY 5

MEDITATION, YOUR KEY TO SUCCESS!

Blessed is the man that walketh not in the counsel of the ungodly, nor standeth in the way of the sinners, nor sitteth in the seat of the scornful. But this delight is in the law of the LORD; and in his law doth he meditate day and night.

PSALMS 1:1,2

Man you've really improved your shot!" Juan exclaimed, "You're just nailing 'em!"
John grinned. "Yeah, man, I've been doing a lot, but not just shooting hoops."
"What else?"
"Well, Mr. Roberts suggested I start meditating to help improve my game."
"Really?'
"Yeah, he told me to keep repeating Philippians 4: 13 over and over: 'I can do all things through Christ which strengthens me.' It has really helped. The concentration helped me to focus better when I play. But even more, thinking about Scriptures has made me pay more attention to living my life for God each moment."

Having godly success in life comes through meditating on God's Word. Meditation isn't a scary thing; it's as if your mind stuck on one thing. When you do this with the Word of God, it will turn your life around and cause you to experience goodness! It's what God promised in Scripture, and that same promise still applies to us today.

God told his people to meditate day and night. This is something that you have to make a commitment to do during your entire life. Simply get your Bible, find meaningful Scriptures that speak to your situation, and think about these passages over and over. Add meditation to your daily regimen of techniques we have talked about this week, and watch God's success track you down and take you over!

APPLICATION

Don't allow yourself the option of failure. Take the top three toughest issues in your life right now. Sit down with your Bible and find three Scriptures that speak to those situations. Memorize those Scriptures. Begin repeating each one in your mind. Use your spare time, shower time, and quiet time to repeat the passages. Watch how God brings answers you need into your life and how he helps you live each day for him.

PRAYER

Father, I need your focus in my life. Please help me to discipline myself enough to meditate day and night on your holy Word. I want everything that I do to be focused on you, and I'm trusting you to help me. In Jesus' name. Amen.

GETTING THE BEST START POSSIBLE

January

Francis Jefferson

Day 1 / Temptation : Working for All the Wrong Reasons

Pray that ye enter not into temptation.

LUKE 22:40

Terry's reward for learning how to type excellent business letters was a telephone call from the personnel manager at the local bank. Terry was hired as a drive-thru teller after the bank manager had received Terry's letter and looked at her qualifications. The job, while starting at minimum wage, would help her to save money for a car and insurance.

On Terry's first day on the job, she met Susan. Later, after Terry completed her training. Susan became her mentor. The two ate lunch together, driving in Susan's beautiful car. Terry spoke admiringly about Susan's car. Susan told her that she could have a car a whole lot faster if Terry pocketed coins from every deposit involving change. Susan said clients did not miss small change and that it was very easy to do. Susan said her first week doing the "change thing" netted her sixty dollars extra.

The possibility of having an automobile can be exciting. When beginning a new job and working for minimum wage, it is difficult to be patient. Realize that it may take time to accomplish all that you would like. However, as a child of God, you must go back to one of the first prayers learned, the Lord's Prayer, particularly the verse that says, "and lead us not into temptation, but deliver us from evil" (Matthew 6: 13).

Make sure that you are not working for the wrong reasons. You must remember that the opportunity to be employed is not a given, but a gift. Look around you and see all of the unemployment. Your ethic should reflect your appreciation of God's gift to you. In return for your gift from God, you should live up to the commitment made when you entered the employer-employee relationship. "Pray that ye enter not into temptation" (Luke 22: 40). If you yield to temptation, you are letting God know that you really do not trust in him for the increase and that you cannot be trusted with his gift of a job. You are taking his gift for granted.

APPLICATION

As you start your day, pause to consider possible distractions that may influence you to yield to temptation. Write down Luke 22:40 on an index card and carry it with you. Pray that you will not fall into temptation through any distraction. Before you leave your house, ask God for strength not to yield to sin.

PRAYER

Father, I thank you for the knowledge and skills that have prepared me to accept a position in the workforce. I recognize that I have some weaknesses. I ask that you will keep your arms of love wrapped around me so that I may be strengthened in tempting situations and may be guided by you. Help me to behave in such a way that others will know not to try to tempt me, for they will recognize that my steps are guided according to your Word. In the name of the victory of your Son, Jesus Christ! Amen.

DAY 2

OBEDIENCE: GIRL, GET A GRIP!

See then that ye walk circumspectly, not as fools, but as wise.

EPHESIANS 5:15

Upon graduating at the top of her class from Harvard University, Karen was invited to interview with a large corporation. Her credentials were outstanding, and the company hired her and then anxiously waited for her to train in the position of junior analyst.

Karen arrived at the office on Monday morning earlier than expected. Before visiting the personnel department, she immediately set her purse and briefcase in an empty office with beautiful furniture and a wonderful view. The chair behind the desk was arranged so that, when seated, you could see a little of the ocean and a touch of the mountains. In personnel, Karen was introduced to her new director, who escorted her to her workstation: a desk up against a wall in a cubicle. Without hesitation, Karen told the director that she preferred the desk in the office She reminded him that she was a top graduate of Harvard. He replied, "Perhaps, one day."

Karen's first assignment included analyzing spreadsheets. After two weeks on the job, she complained about doing them. She told the director that she felt it was unfair for her to continue such menial work. She did not spend four years at Harvard to end up wasting her talent looking at spreadsheets. After six months on the job, Karen was asked to leave.

Girl, get a grip. You must be aware that every organization has criteria that determine where employees will fit in the office structure. It has been said that opportunities come to those who wait. Be careful how you behave—not as a fool.

Don't let your impression of yourself overwhelm you and lead you to believe you can be disobedient. Just because you attend a good school, come from a particular family, or personally know the company owner, your accomplishments are the gift of God. "For we are his workmanship, created in Christ Jesus unto good works, which God hath before ordained that we should walk in them." (Ephesians 2: 10). If you are obedient, rewards will come in the form of bonuses and promotions. Who knows? One day you may become the employer and make the decisions on who gets to work in the best office space.

APPLICATION

Be obedient. Do the work you are given, without complaint. Earn your rewards; don't expect them to be handed to you.

PRAYER

Father, you have given me many opportunities. For those , I pause to say thank you. Keep me humble, so that I may show my appreciation to you and to those who have been patient with me. Help me to understand that I am not all that I should be, and bless me to get to where you want me to be. I ask this and all other blessings in the name of your Son, Jesus. Amen.

DAY 3

ENDURANCE: WHEN PUSH COMES TO SHOVE

For whatsoever things were written aforetime were written for our learning, that we through patience and comfort of the scriptures might have hope.

ROMANS 15:4

Faith was sixteen years old. Because of some conflicts in her home and school life, she had decided to drop out of school. Now she was participating in Job Corps, a training program offering youth in Faith's situation the opportunity to receive a small salary and learn a technical skill while completing a GED.

One evening, Faith was standing around with friends on the Job Corps campus. A security guard, patrolling the campus, noticed the gathering and got out of his car to make sure that everything was on the up-and-up. As he approached, he noticed the smell of marijuana in the air. Faith was one of the first to speak up to defend herself, insisting that she was not partaking. However, when tested, the results were positive. Job Corps has a no-tolerance policy, and Faith's future was on the line. Faith knew the disappointment her parents would feel. She was in a push-comes-to-shove-situation. She requested a hearing but was denied the opportunity.

Something youth generally learn too late is that they will be judged by the company they keep. Thus, they should make every effort to examine their friends and coworkers. Young people may need to make some changes in their relationships.

If you walk by faith, unfavorable situations in your life can change. By faith, we understand that the worlds were framed by the Word of God. By faith, Enoch left this life, but he did not experience death. By faith, Noah built an ark to save his family. By faith, Abraham went out to a land he did not know. By faith, Sara, though old and barren, was able to conceive a child (Hebrews 11:3, 5, 7, 8, 11).

APPLICATION

Today, when you find yourself in a when-push-comes-to-shove situation, take the time to whisper a little prayer that God will help you use the faith within yourself to make the right decisions.

PRAYER

Father, there are so many challenges that confront me. Lord, help me to depend upon you and you alone so that I can grow stronger in faith. Thank you for the lessons I have learned from the mistakes that I have made. Strengthen me when I am weak and give me a sense of direction so that I may make the best decision when it comes to my desires and goals. I ask you for the victory. Amen.

DAY 4

DISCOURAGEMENT: DON'T EVEN GO THERE!

Be strong and of good courage, and do it: fear not, nor be dismayed: for the LORD God, even my God, will be with thee; he will not fail thee, nor forsake thee, until thou hast finished all the work for service of the house of the LORD.

1 CHRONICLES 28:20

Sherlyn was totally discouraged when she arrived at work on Monday morning. It had been one of those weekends that had left her drained. On Friday night, she loaned her car to her boyfriend. His transmission had gone out and he told her he needed to borrow her car to go to work. Sherlyn spent Saturday morning working on bills, trying to balance her checkbook. She had overestimated her income and was going to be unable to pay all the bills and have enough money to make it until the next paycheck.

Her boyfriend did not call until Sunday. He promised that he would pick her up Monday morning, but when she tried to call him after she got dressed for work, he was nowhere to be found. She ended up having to catch the bus and arrived 45 minutes late when it was her responsibility to open. As a result, her superior reprimanded her. Sherlyn responded with anger and excuses and was placed on probation.

We have a tendency to become discouraged when our lives do not "go like clockwork." We blame others for what we are feeling. We are not motivated to do our best work, and others often have to pick up the slack. Despite what is going on in your personal life, you have a responsibility to give your best on the job. It is not your boss's problem if you don't have a ride to work or if you are not budgeting to make ends meet. When blessed with a job and rewarded with a paycheck, you have a responsibility to manage the funds according to what you know that you will receive.

APPLICATION

Make it a point to get a good night's sleep this evening. Before you start your day tomorrow say, "Lord, there is no way I will be discouraged. I am too blessed. If, by chance, I make bad choices with my blessing, I will repent and turn to you. Then, I can sing and make music in my heart to you, giving thanks for all things." (See Ephesians 5: 19, 20)

PRAYER

Father, you have blessed me abundantly and for that I am thankful. Help me to make good choices so that I may continue to share my blessings. Help me to be mindful of how and with who I share them. Give me the motivation, Father, to look to thee in moments of discouragement. Thank you for all that you are in my life. Give me the victory, I pray! Amen.

DAY 5
HONESTLY: TRUTH OR CONSEQUENCES

Finally, Brethren, whatsoever things are true, whatsoever things are honest, whatsoever things are just, whatsoever things are pure, whatsoever things are lovely, whatsoever things are of good report, if there be any virtue, and if there be any praise, think on these things.

PHILIPPIANS 4:8

Camille worked hard in school looking forward to the opportunity to secure the job of her dreams: one with excellent vacation benefits, a good health plan, other insurance, and stock options that would secure her future. She was elated when that opportunity came from a large, established corporation with thousands of employees, a corporation she believed had good work ethics.

Imagine her surprise when, a few years later, the company faced serious financial problems because of unethical accounting practices. Nearly one thousand employees, including Camille, were laid off. She lost her investments, all because honesty was not in her company's work ethic. The company's failure to tell the truth caused many to suffer terrible consequences.

Because we have human tendencies, we put our trust in corporations, organizations, and individuals. We will trust them with our money, our life, and our treasured secrets. Why do you think this is? How many times has a friend shared something with you and said to you, "If I tell you this, can I trust you not to tell anyone?" Your response is probably "Yes, honest, you can trust me." Your excitement from just hearing the secret leads you to tell someone else and that person promises not to tell anyone. Before you know it, the secret becomes the subject of office gossip.

It is your fault. You were dishonest. You betrayed a friend, and that friend is now embarrassed and hurt. When people are not honest in thoughts, words, and deeds, they have failed to consider the consequences. Remember Philippians 4: 8 and live accordingly.

APPLICATION

This day, make honesty part of your work and personal ethic. Do not cheat, lie, or steal in any situation.

PRAYER

Dear Lord, give me strength to keep my head up and remain honest. Help me to be aware that I must always stand for honesty and tell the truth in order that others do not suffer consequences because of me. I pray that my honesty will shine as an example for others and that, through me, they might see your light and know that they, too, can stand the test. Give me the victory, I pray! Amen.

Daily Devotions

GETTING THE BEST START POSSIBLE

January

WEEK THREE: HEALTH

Patrice Elliot-Mace

Day 1 / Take Care of What God Provided for You

*Beloved, I wish above all things that thou mayest prosper
and be in health, even as thy soul prospereth.*

3 JOHN 1:2

It was just a few days after New Year's, and all Estell could think about was what wasn't going right in her life. Estell's sophomore year of high school had started out fine until she decided to hang out with a new bunch of friends. Chillin' with her crew was fun—Estell never knew what they were going to get into next. Estell's new friends liked to smoke, drink, and party. Soon, Estell picked up her friends' habits and even passed out cold at a party from too much alcohol. By years end, Estell's mother had to get her into a group for teens who were abusing alcohol.

How did things get so messed up? Estell asked herself one morning. *All I wanted to do was have some fun and hang out with my new friends.* There was a knock.

"Estell?" one of her old friends, Shantay was at her bedroom door. "Would you let me in?" Estell forced herself to get up and open the door. "Estell, you mom told me about the problems you are going through. You have to remember that you can turn things around from here. Let's pray about it," Shantay said encouragingly.

———————

Our bodies must be vessels to the Lord. They must be that special place where we welcome God's presence and where his Holy Spirit dwells. Honor God by developing a healthy lifestyle that will aid your growth and development. It is your responsibility to take care of the treasure that is your body, a gift from God.

APPLICATION

Begin each day thanking God for the body he has provided you. Eat nutritiously and include fitness in your daily activities. Stay away from substances that would destroy your health. Become involved in activities that allow your spiritual life and self-confidence to grow, using the gifts that God has given you.

PRAYER

Most merciful and loving Father, thank you for health, strength, and countless blessings of which I will never be worthy. Help me, Lord to honor you by caring for my mind, body, and soul. In the blessed name of Jesus, I pray. Amen.

Day 2
FOLLOWING GOD'S TEACHINGS

Be Not wise in thine own eyes: fear the LORD, and depart from evil.
It shall be health to thy navel, and marrow to thy bones.

PROVERBS 3:7,8

Getting good grades in school had been important to Yvonne since elementary school. She discovered that she didn't need to study hard to end up near the top of her class. All that mattered to her was outdoing everyone else.

As the top student in all of her classes, Yvonne made her classmates feel dumb. Whenever other students had trouble answering a teacher's question, Yvone would embarrass them in front of the class.

Due to Yvonne's attitude, her classmates did not want anything to do with her. She had a lot going for her, but no one would ever find that out.

Even Christians can be caught up in all the worldly hype. We can begin to act as if we are self-made and any success we experience in life is purely our doing. Such thinking is not good for us. It is the gospel of Jesus Christ and his way of living that

makes us healthy. Be mindful that "The fear of the LORD is the beginning of wisdom and the knowledge of the holy is understanding" (Proverbs 9:10). At any time, our lives, health or circumstances can change for the worse. We thrive because it is God's will and not because we are so worthy. Since only God is wise, we should thank God for a healthy mind and body to do his will.

APPLICATION

Young women, offer to God a prayer of thanksgiving for health, strength, and a sound mind. In a journal, make a list of seven health-related blessings for which you are grateful.

PRAYER

Oh Lord, how excellent is thy name in all the earth! We thank you, Lord, for health and strength. How blessed we are to be able go about our days. Help us to avoid self-righteousness. In Jesus' name, Amen.

Day 3
UNDERSTAND GOD'S WILL TO LIVE IT

For they are life unto those that find them, and health to all their flesh.

PROVERBS 4:22

For the past three years, Sandra had tried out for the girls' basketball team No matter how much, she practiced, the results were the same: She never made the team. Sandra was starting to wonder whether she should even bother trying.

"Look, Sandra" Keona said. "I think you should try again. You never know, this could be the year you make it."

"I'm not sure, Keona. Last time I go so nervous before the tryouts that I had an upset stomach and my nerves were shot. My playing showed it."

"First, we need to work on your attitude. You'll never make the cut if you don't believe in yourself," Keona said. "What I want you to do is pray about your making the team. Next, starting each morning, I want you to read your Bible and pray. The last thing you have to do is prepare for tryouts with lots of practice."

Keona prayed and prayed with Sandra and reminded her of what she had promised to do. Sandra practiced and prayed hard. By the time tryouts came, she felt prepared and confident that, if it were God's will, she would make the team. And no matter what, she did her best this time because she wasn't nervous. She had put things in God's hands.

Sisters, we must understand what our Lord expects of us and work at living within his will. Our obedience will result in the blessings of a healthy and productive life. "The way of the LORD is strength to the upright: but destruction shall be the workers of iniquity." (Proverbs 10: 29) if we ignore our Lord's teachings, we invite the potential for negativity and doubt, which break down a sound mind and a healthy body.

APPLICATION

Young women, make an appointment with your doctor to map out your health strategy for your nutritional, physical, and emotional health requirements.

PRAYER

Father God, I praise you. I realize that no task, problem, or challenge will ever be too great for you to handle. Please free me from any depressive or destructive behavior that is barring me from achieving a healthy and godly lifestyle. Amen.

Day 4

SEEK GOD'S WORD SO YOU WILL FLOURISH

That thy way may be known up earth, thy saving health among all nations.

PSALM 67:2

It was difficult for Sara to hear her dad say that he didn't understand why she, her mother, and her sister went to church each Sunday. Sara's dad was having some major issues in his life, which were causing a lot of strain on all his relationships, including his relationship with Christ. He just didn't see how God or church was relevant in his life. No matter what they did, he would never come to church, even for major holidays. In spite of this, Sara's mom prepared for church on Sunday mornings by tuning on her favorite gospel radio station and making breakfast. After the girls got dressed, they would pile in the car and be on their way to church.

"Mommy," Sara's little sister asked one Sunday. "Why doesn't Daddy go to church?"
"Because he and God have not wrestled through his issues yet," replied Mom.
"You know what, Mom?" Sara said, "I think I'll pray for Dad."

Beloved, how blessed we are to be able to study the Bible so we might learn what the Lord has said. If we don't know the Word, we can be led into evil. Remember to "Seek ye first the kingdom of God, and his righteousness; and all these things shall

be added unto you" (Matthew 6:33). A by-product of our salvation is the blessing of good health, a sound mind, and a spirit focused on a disciplined lifestyle.

APPLICATION

Today, vow not to let anyone else's behavior stress you.

PRAYERS

Father, show me how to live a better life through the study and understanding of your holy Word. As I strive to follow your teachings, help me to put into practice your plan for a healthy Christian lifestyle. Amen.

Day 5
JESUS WILL HEAL YOU

For I will restore health unto thee, and I will heal thee of they wounds,
saith the Lord; because they called thee an Outcast, saying,
This is Zion, whom no man worketh after.

JEREMIAH 30:17

The gossip around school said that Vernita had been with most of the boys on the football team. She was the talk of the boys' locker room, and many of the girls would not have anything to do with her. Other students laughed, whispered, and pointed at her. One day she overheard a conversation in the girls' restroom.

"Michael told me that he heard that Vernita slept with him," Cynthia said to Terri. "It's no surprise to me," Terri said.

Another girl came out of a stall in the bathroom, washed her hands, and said to Vernita, "You know there's a foul smell in here. Lets go, Vernita."

After they walked out of the bathroom, Vernita asked, "Why did you do that? Most kids at school avoid me."

The girl stated, "First of all, my name is Sierra, they call me Cici. Second, I feel it's not fair to judge someone on hearsay. I am a Christian and I believe in giving everyone a chance; after all, Jesus does it for me all the time."

"What should I do Cici? Some of the things they say about me are true. And it's all very upsetting. I can barely eat, and I'm not sleeping well," Vernita responded.

"I will pray for you, but I want you to ask God for his forgiveness and the strength to deal with the situation at school. I also think you should take advantage of the counseling services offered by the community center. I have. God will see you through this and I will be there for support," Cici said.

APPLICATION

No matter where you've been or what you've done with your life, you are never out of the reach of God's love and forgiveness. If you have been hurt emotionally or physically, God can heal you. Jesus said, "I am come that they might have life, and that they might have it more abundantly" (John 10: 10). Thank you, God!

Today, young women attend church as well as fitness, nutrition and emotional support classes to work on building up your self-esteem and getting in touch with the Holy Spirit. Engage in activities that build up your self-confidence.

PRAYER

Blessed Jesus, thank you for loving me just as I am. Please forgive me for when I have failed to live the kind of life that would be pleasing in your sight. Give me the determination and discipline I need. Amen.

GETTING THE BEST START POSSIBLE

January

WEEK FOUR: SELF-ESTEEM

Monique Headley

Day 1 / David's Slingshot—Stand and Deliver the Word

But the LORD, said unto me, Say not, I am a child: for thou shalt go to all that I shall send thee, and whatsoever I commanded thee thou shalt speak. Be not afraid of their faces: for I am with thee to deliver thee, saith the Lord.

JEREMIAH 1:7,8

As the only committed Christian on the Valentine's Day Dance planning committee, Riley felt dejected after the last meeting. The committee wanted to make sure the dance was a purely fun event, complete with a shake-what-ya-mama-gave-ya dance contest. Riley felt it would be more appropriate if the event wasn't so wild but instead included an abstinence pledge ceremony.

Popular opinion was worldlier. The other students didn't want to give her idea much weight, and Riley felt unsure of how to change their minds. Faced with the decision to quit or stay on and try to persuade the other students, Riley was at a crossroads. Her decision would have an impact on how she would be perceived and received. On behalf of the Lord, would her decision be to fight or take flight?

Our honest responsibilities and decisions are more telling of our personal convictions than our words, as they reveal our beliefs with crystal clarity. Life as a daughter of God—a Christian woman—will provide plenty of trials and tribulations for such revelations. How are we to respond? Are we to profess the glory of the Lord only when we know it will be easily received and be silent when we know we might have to explain? It is important that we fight the good fight—always, not according to convenience. The power of the Lord will guide you to where you are supposed to be, when you are supposed to be there, and instruct you on what you are supposed to do and say.

———————

As Shadrach, Meshach, and Abednego (Daniel 3: 13-30) were spared the flames of the fire after refusing to serve any ideal other than what they knew to be the truth, so too should you be bold. The strength of the Lord will protect you. The wisdom of the Lord will guide you. As Christian women, we must continue to be guided and, in turn, guide others to higher ground. Besides, our mommas know what they gave us, and I bet they never wanted it to be shaken, anyway. Tell somebody about the goodness of the Lord.

APPLICATION

When you are faced with a challenging situation in which others are not open to your ideas or your Christian ideals, take the time to speak with them one-in-one. A relationship with God is a personal decision and you must be respectful of others opinions. Speak with them about how Jesus changed your life and how they could benefit from the same gift. Let them know that you are available to talk about Him and then let them make their own decision. The choice is theirs but you can be the one to show them the way. Don't give up, but don't sacrifice your ideals either. If you find yourself in a situation of unconscionable compromise, find like-minded Christian women and hold onto your faith.

PRAYER

Lord, I ask that you guide me on my journey and give me the strength to be who you need me to be so that I may spread your Word as far as possible, until my last breath. Where you lead, I will follow and encourage others to do the same. I love you, Lord. Amen.

Day 2

HARD-PRESSED, YET BLESSED
—SELF CONFIDENCE

But we have this treasure in earthen vessels, that the excellence of the
power may be of God, and not of us. We are troubled on every side,
yet not distressed; we are perplexed, but not in despair; Persecuted,
but not forsaken; cast down, but not destroyed;
Always bearing about in the body the dying of the Lord Jesus,
that the life also of Jesus might be made manifest in our mortal flesh.

2 CORINTHIANS 4:7-10

While Tory recuperated in the hospital, all she could think about was money and specifically from where it would come. Tory was afraid of how much it was going to cost for the medical care and hospital stay, as well as the car repairs after the accident (thank God she hadn't hurt anybody). There were all the other bills that were in her name and sitting on her dresser at home. Despite the lingering pain, all she could think about was returning to work so that she could start reducing her debt that was accumulating minute by minute.

On the verge of tears, it was then that Tory turned her head to see the sun break through the clouds and burst into her room. In all the sky, that one ray shone for Tory and illuminated the Bible on her bed table. In that moment, Tory was reminded that with God's grace and unwavering faith in Him, she would be capable of handling anything that came her way. As Tory reached for her Bible, the confidence in her smile returned.

As with cherries, roses, and fire, there is sweetness and pits, fragrance and thorns, illumination and pain. With life, there is good and bad. While we may not be in control of our destinies or determine the trials we go through on earth, we do hold the key to our experience. "God chooses what we go through; we choose how we go through it," says leadership expert John C. Maxwell. That's it in a nutshell; The keys to our experience are, first, our belief in God; second, belief in self; and finally, finally, outlook on life.

As Christian women, accustomed to God's miraculous power, we know the possibility of an impossible situation. When hard-pressed and confronted with a trying situation, we must search for our ray of sunshine and know always that our God will give us the power to accomplish all in His will. God is good, indeed.

APPLICATION

Think of a time when you have had an impossible situation and how you were able to find God's ray of hope in the midst of it.

PRAYER

Lord, I thank you for making me so strong. I thank you for challenging me to overcome and achieve more than I ever thought possible. I thank you for every lesson. I know that you have given me what I need for my journey, and though I am tested, I know I have the tools to triumph. In your name, I claim my victory. I love you, Lord. Amen

Day 3
WHAT SELF-RESPECTING WOMAN WON'T STAND

Thou art all fair, my love; there is no spot in thee.

SONG OF SOLOMON 4:7

Maya's parents didn't like Derek, but she was hooked. He was a bit rough around the edges, but Maya liked a challenge. Even though he sometimes got angry with her and seemed on the edge of exploding even for little things, she felt he would never do anything bad to her. Though her parents saw it, love blinded her to Derek's abusive potential and they continued to date.

At the church picnic, she hadn't meant to spill salad dressing on his suit, but the spoon had slipped. Without thinking, Derek lashed out and caller her a name she never thought she would hear him say. Immediately he tried to apologize, but the spell was broken. Through her heartbreak, Maya knew that surely this man was not the one the Lord meant for her.

God's love for us is perfect and unwavering, no matter what we do. As Christian women, we know that there will never be a love stronger than the love of God for his creations. Though early love is imperfect, it is a precious gift. At it's best, it is nurturing, never cruel. Above all, love never crushes those for whom it claims to care.

As we search for love, we must seek out the best that God offers on earth. Love is a jewel to be nestled between our hearts and that of our beloved's, to be carefully protected, and to serve as a rock in an unshakable foundation. Love is a coveted prize that will encourage us, let us know we are special, support us, and treat us as the unique treasures we are.

APPLICATION

From this day forward take a stand for yourself by vowing not to listen to music, watch programs, or interact with people that disrespect women.

PRAYER

Lord, I ask that you make me a humble servant who walks in your ways. I ask that if it is your will, you grant me a husband who will cherish and love me with all of his heart. I will follow where you guide me, will not be influenced by my own selfish desires, and will wait patiently, I love you Lord, Amen.

Day 4

SISTAFRIENDS HAVE A DUTY TO TREAT YOU RIGHT

And Delilah said to Samson, Tell me, I pray thee, wherein thy great strength lithe, and wherewith thou mightest be bound to afflict thee.

JUDGES 16:6

Though they had just met a few days earlier at the Sistafriend Networking conference, Dana was willing to tell Marina all her secrets—things she hadn't told to anyone else, even her family. The two young women seemed to hit it off so easily. It had been a while since Dana last had a girlfriend who she really trusted. Marina seemed to be that trustworthy.

Though Marina promised to keep her secrets confidential at the next conference meeting. Dana noticed that the other women now seemed a bit distant. When Dana caught up with Marina, she asked if she had said anything to the other women. Glancing away nervously, Marina said unconvincingly that she had kept her promise but Dana had a sinking feeling in her stomach that the other woman was not telling the truth.

Best girlfriends are better than apple pie. They are comforting and cozy, remind you of sitting in a warm kitchen surrounded by love. They are a sweet de-stressor in tough times. However, when you have a bad apple in your apple pie, you have

something altogether different. We must have a spirit of discernment at all times, especially when it comes to confidantes.

It's not smart to tell all your business. It's not wise to entrust others with powerful personal information. Nevertheless, sometimes, we do it. Why do we feel we have to give it all up? Are we being too needy? Shouldn't we be turning to God first? Are we trying to make friends in an attempt to be liked? Of course, have friends and turn to them, as you need. However, do so only after you have confirmed their intentions. Not everyone should have access to your inner sanctum. Not everyone is worthy of knowing your precious thoughts.

APPLICATION

When you feel the need to confide in a girlfriend, make it a point to speak to God first. You may avoid the need to visit the sister-friend confessional booth. As you make friends, take them into your confidence only after you know them to be worthy. Spend time with them, chitchat, and gradually increase their security-clearance status in your life. If they do not pass the test, dishonorably discharge them.

PRAYER

Lord, I ask that you give me a spirit of discernment in my life. I ask that you guide me to the right people and places and save me from harm—verbal, physical, and spiritual. Keep me safe from those who will not do me right and protect me in all that I do. I love you, Lord. Amen.

Day 5

GOD'S HIGH FASHION-
OOO-LA-LA LORD?

*But the Lord said unto Samuel, Look not on his countenance,
or on the height of his stature; because I have refused him:
for the Lord seeth not as man seeth; for man looketh on the outward
appearance, but the Lord looketh on the heart.*

1 SAMUEL 16:7

Aneika always prided herself on being the best dresser in the choir. Hair done, nails done—she looked perfect. Aneika also liked to wear the fashions from the magazines, sometimes even if it was cut up to here or dipped down to there. Folks liked to talk about her style-gone-wrong; all her good deeds went unnoticed because of the gossip.

Aneika didn't want to dress like an old frump, but she didn't want folks to be distracted by her clothes and miss who she really was—a good Christian woman who had a little bit of style going on. Aneika loved the Lord and wanted to dress his vessel in finery. She just had to remember to always dress his vessel with discretion.

Divas don't have to dress drearily, however, they should always dress respectfully. Vanity is disrespectful of the Lord and attracts the wrong kind of attention from others. A sense of style is fine, but we should always be respectful of our bodies. The wrong kind of attention signals that we might be contestants in the Ms. I need-to-be-noticed pageant. We're not exactly going to win any self-confidence awards wearing that sash! We should express our style in a way that best represents us. Respect your body; it's a precious gift from God. Dress it as if you mean what you pray.

APPLICATION

Today, examine your wardrobe. A good rule of thumb is for clothing to be well constructed and fit your measurements. Avoid clothing that is too tight or too short or has peekaboo holes or no midriff. You should dress to show the respect you have for your body, yourself, and your God.

PRAYER

Lord, I thank you for the gifts you have given me. I do not consider them casually. I have high regard for myself and would never want to appear otherwise. I seek your guidance in all that I do so that I may live, dress, walk, and talk rightly. Above all, I pray that I am more beautiful on the inside than I could ever be on the outside. I love you, Lord. Amen

GETTING THE BEST START POSSIBLE

January

Vanessa Salami

Day 1 / Mariah's Story

And David behaved himself wisely in all his ways; and the Lord was with him.

1 SAMUEL 18:14

Mariah and Arielle stepped down from their ride, dancing, singing, and blowing kisses to the city bus as it pulled away. Arielle hugged her friend and said,, "You did it! I am so proud of you! You are the girl!" Mariah stood at attention and began speaking into her soda bottle, "First of all I would like to thank..." Both of them started laughing.

Mariah and Arielle were returning from an audition for an upcoming play. Mariah had gotten the lead role. Mariah was sad that her best friend did not get a part, but Arielle was not the least bit mad, sad, or jealous. She was very happy for Mariah.

Mariah had faced a lot of pressure at school and at home but still managed to get good grades, be active in the youth group, and live up to her responsibilities. Mariah said that she started each day by greeting God and asking him to lead her in everything that she would do during the day.

Just as David was a man after God's own heart, God is searching the earth today for those whose hearts are sold out to him. Young women whose hearts are filled with the love of God are rare jewels in schools, homes and communities. Their light will draw others who will want to know what the secret is. These young ladies will be respected and admired by friends and family.

Television tells young people that success is all about knowing the right people in Hollywood, New York, and other such places. Simply looking at the lives of many famous actresses and singers shows that worldly success is temporary and often leaves people disappointed and bitter. True success—the kind that lasts for all eternity—is about knowing and living with the right one, God.

APPLICATION

It is time to find out what has captivated your heart. Get seven sheets of paper. Label each sheet a different day off the week. Divide each sheet into three sections. In the first section, write morning. In the next section, put down the very first thought that come to your mind that day. In the second section, jot down what you focused on during the middle of the day. In the third section, list what occupied your heart in the evening. After one week, read all the sheets and determine whether you need to ask God to help you make him the major focus of your life.

PRAYER

Our Father who art in heaven, thank you for your grace. Thank you for breathing life into me. Thank you, Father, for being my Father and my friend. Thank you for giving me passion for life. And thank you, Father, for making a way for me to be successful in the things you put in my heart. I pray this prayer in the name of the King of Kings, Jesus Christ. Amen.

Day 2
DEANNA'S DAYS

Wherefore when Saul saw that he behaved himself very wisely,
he was afraid of him.

1 SAMUEL 18:15

Sonya brushed against Deanna, making her drop her math and science books. As Deanna kneeled to pick them up, Sonya whispered, "Why don't you go back to where you came from?"

Deanna stood to her five-foot-ten stature and said in her Ghanian accent, "The only thing that matters in life is where you're going. Nobody can ever go back."

Sonya said, "I bet I can make you go back and visit that floor again." Sonya had always been the most popular girl in school. Once Deanna came, that all changed. Deanna had been an orphan back in African. To this day she did not know who purchased her airplane tickets why she was allowed to leave the country, or how she ended up in the home of a loving, God-fearing family.

Because of the blessings God bestowed in her life, Deanna decided to glorify him in all that she did. At school, she participated well in her classes, she helped the basketball team win many games, and she was selected hostess of the senior class dance. That was the final straw for Sonya, who began tormenting Deanna. However, Deanna believed that even in this, God would be glorified.

People will be jealous of your success. Why? Because when they see you, they will see their own lack of achievement. Young ladies can take classes that enhance their skills and talents to achieve the dreams that have been put in their hearts by God. Many young women, however, don't realize their capabilities, nor do they ask for God's help in living a life for him. Failing to do your best because you don't want to hurt someone else is dishonorable to God. Use what God has blessed you with to honor him, and you will be able to touch the stars.

APPLICATION

What direction are you headed in right now? Get your last three report cards from school. Have your grades gone up or down? Locate your checkbook, coin jar, or whatever you use to hold your money. Count it. Has the amount gone up or down over the last three months? Think about the ministries you participate in at church. Have your activities helped to grow the ministry? For any areas where you are at a standstill or going backwards, write down the reasons you are not moving forward by answering the following questions: 1) What am I afraid of losing by moving ahead? 2) What do I need to learn or study in order to move forward? 3) What do I need to ask God for to help me move ahead?

PRAYER

Dear Father, please take control of every area of my life. Please work through me, so that others can see your glory. Soften the heart of anyone who may be jealous or envious of the work you do in me. In the name of my Lord and Savior, your Son, Jesus Christ. Amen.

Day 3
NICHOLE'S NATURAL KNOCK

If the iron be blunt, and he do not whet the edge, then must he put to more strength: but wisdom is profitable to direct.

ECCLESIASTES 10:10

Nichole rang her parents' doorbell, anxious to tell them the great news. Nichole's parents wanted her to be a doctor. Her college expenses had cost a fortune, and her parents had helped pay them by each working two jobs. Studying did not come easy for Nichole. In fact, hitting the books was often the last thing she wanted to do. Adding art classes to her schedule made it a lot easier, however.

Nichole believed that she would make an adequate rather than superb doctor. What Nichole loved to do was paint. She lived and breathed art. That's all she wanted to do, but how could she ever tell her parents?

Nicholes's mother came to the door. "Hey, sweetie!"
"Mom, I have some great news. My paintings were on display at the Expo Gallery for the past two weeks..."
"I know," cut in Nichole's mother. "Seeing them made me realize that an artist is what you were meant to be. Give it everything you've got, baby."

Do you know anybody who is naturally good at something? Maybe one of your girlfriends is the best dancer you have ever seen. What if that dancer never took dance lessons? Do you think she would reach the level of success she was born to have? We must sharpen the abilities that God has given us, with education and practice. We must also remember that our skills are to be used to bring glory to God and not to ourselves.

APPLICATION

It's time to take inventory of your skills and talents. With what natural gifts and talents did the Lord bless you? Write them down. Find someone—a church member, teacher or family member—who has become successful using the same gifts with which you have been blessed. Ask the following questions: 1) What did you do when your were my age that contributed to the success you have today? 2) What classes would you recommend I take? 3) What obstacles could keep me from reaching success? Finally, in your prayers, ask God how he wants you to glorify him with the skill with which he has blessed you.

PRAYER

Most gracious and merciful father, you are the giver of everything. Father grant me the wisdom to know which gifts I should sharpen in order to work for your kingdom. Help me to see how to use my skills to bless others and bring you glory. In the name of the most honorable Son of God. Jesus Christ, I pray. Amen.

Day 4
SUCCESS IN DUE TIME

But thanks be to God, which giveth us the victory
through our Lord Jesus Christ.

1 CORINTHIANS 15:57

Taylor prayed to God every night but it did not seem as though anything changed. Nobody would accept her. Sade and Kierra were eating at the deli at a table near the window. Taylor asked them if she could join them, and they told her yes. As soon as she sat down, they got up.

Taylor had dropped out of high school, had been arrested, and had spent time in jail for crimes she did while hanging with the wrong crowd. Ever since Taylor gave her life to Christ, she was different. Now she was sorry for the things she had done, was finishing night classes to get her GED, and wondered why no one could see that she had changed.

"Hi, Taylor, Do you mind if I sit with you?" Taylor looked up to see Jasmine. Jasmine was a Christian in her GED class. Taylor said yes. Jasmine noticed Taylor's red eyes. Jasmine said, "Don't worry about them, Taylor. God loves you more than anyone on this earth can. You have given him your heart. Trust me, girlfriend, he will give you the victory." The words made Taylor smile.

Some people will just never let you forget the past. Once you accept Jesus Christ as your Lord and Savior, your past is behind you. The only thing is that everybody does not believe or understand that. You may have done some awful things that you regret. But if you are truly sorry and have asked God to forgive you, then you are right with him. Just keep looking ahead to where God wants you to go. Maybe he wants you to use your past experiences to help others avoid the same mistakes. If you keep your eyes ahead and walk hand in hand with Jesus, you are heading toward victory.

APPLICATION

Does something that you did in the past keep coming back to bother you—either by someone reminding you of it or you not being able to let go? If another person won't let you forget, think about the best words to let that person know that God has forgiven you and is leading you down a new path. Practice what you are going to say a couple of times so that you will be at ease. If your own mind won't let you forget the past, whenever a thought comes to mind, begin to ask God for a new mind. Get the thought out of your head by bringing God in and asking for his help.

PRAYER

Dear Father, help me to know that when people turn their backs on me, I can always come to you. Please help me to understand, Lord, that success, joy, and peace can come only through Jesus Christ. In the name of the glorious king, Jesus Christ, I pray. Amen

Day 5
COMMITMENT

Commit thy works unto the Lord, and thy thoughts shall be established.
PROVERBS 16:3

Candace picked up the phone to call her friend Jada. "J, what am I going to do?"

What's up, girl?"

"Mr. Brown just called and told me that he made a big mistake. He said the Jam for Jesus room was already booked for the Brother to Brother concert two months before I asked for it, but somebody forgot to put it on his calendar.

"Wow, that's messed up. Either you're going to have to get another place to have the Girl Rap or reschedule it."

Candace had been planning her Girl Rap weekend for four months. This was an event Candace had dreamed of putting together. She invited all of the teenagers in the neighborhood. Candace had received three hundred calls from people interested in attending. She was going to use the Girl Rap weekend to make her mark as a Christian rapper.

"Candace, how did God answer your prayers about the Girl Rap weekend?" asked Jada. "You did put this into the hands of Jesus, didn't you?"

"J. I have to go, I'll call you later." Candace hung up the phone, fell onto her knees, and asked God to forgive her for not seeking him first. When she stood, she began calling to let everyone know that the Girl Rap weekend was being postponed.

What are some of the biggest plans you have for yourself? Are you determined to go to a particular school? Do you want to throw the best party anyone has ever attended? Is your heart set on becoming famous? Everyone should have a plan for life. It has been said that those who fail to plan, plan to fail. Jesus told us that we should plan before taking action. Your first step in planning activities is to ask God. He said to commit whatever—not some of what—you do for him. Plans that you act on without consulting God may be for your own glory or selfish desires. Why would or should God bless what you're doing? Seeking God will help you realize the true intentions of your plans.

APPLICATION

Get a beautiful sheet of stationery. On the top, write: PLANS I COMMIT TO MY FATHER. Write on that sheet everything that you are giving to God. Tape it to your mirror or another place that you look at each day. Each day, read it to remind yourself that God is in control of your life. As plans happen, take them off the list and add new ones.

PRAYER

My merciful Father in heaven, this day I commit all of my plans, hopes, and desires to you. I commit my career choice, education, and all of my relationships into your hands. Father, I am yours, direct me, as you will. In the most majestic name of Jesus Christ, I pray. Amen.

Daily Devotions

WHAT GOD SAYS ABOUT LOVE
February

WEEK ONE: Friendships

Chandra Sparks Taylor

Day 1 / What about Your Friends?

Faithful are the wounds of a friend; but the kisses of an enemy are deceitful.
PROVERBS 27:6

Nia had met her best friend, Jessica, in seventh grade. From the moment they were introduced, they were inseparable. Even though they had different schedules, they ate lunch together and talked on the phone. Outside school, when you saw one, you saw the other—until they had a huge argument over cheerleading and stopped speaking.

Soon after, Jessica was leaving school and found Nia in the bathroom crying. Forgetting their argument, she quickly went to comfort her friend. "What's wrong, Jess?

"I found out I made the cheerleading squad."
"That's great," Nia said, truly happy for her friend. "But why are you crying?"

"Well, I was so excited when I got the news. I couldn't wait to tell you, but then I remembered that we weren't talking. When I had asked your advice about my routine and you have me your honest opinion, I didn't want to hear it. That's why I got mad. But I took your advice, and now I made the squad. Have I lost you?

It pays to pick your friends wisely. True friends will not tell you what you want to hear; they will tell you the truth, no matter how much it hurts. Although we may not always want to hear it, knowing that someone has your back and is going to be there for you—despite who you are and what you are going through—is comforting. True friendship, like true love, stands the test of time. Make sure that you choose wisely when you choose your friends.

APPLICATION

Today, make a list of all of your friends. Examine your list honestly and eliminate all those who have talked about you behind your back, lied to you, laughed about you, or done things that were not in your best interest. How many people are left? Take the time today write each true friend a short note thanking her for her friendship.

PRAYER

Lord, thank you for surrounding me with people who love and care about me, in spite of my faults. Bless me to be the kind of friend I want others to be to me. In thy darling Son Jesus' name, I pray. Amen.

Day 2
WHOM DO YOU RESPECT

*Make no friendship with an angry man; and with a furious man
thou shalt not go: lest thou learn his ways, and get a snare to thy soul.*

PROVERBS 22:24,25

Jessica was on a natural high. She had cheered at her first game of the season, and the football team had won. She drove home to change. As she got dressed, she thought about the squad. They were so cool. They always wore the latest fashions and all the other kids idolized them. Then she thought about how some of the cheerleaders talked down to other kids at school.

Shame filled Jessica's heart when she remembered how the cheerleaders had teased one girl for wearing no-name clothes. The squad leader had said some very nasty things. Other members of the squad, including Jessica, had joined in. It had seemed harmless until the girl started crying. Then Jessica wished she could apologize.

————

Sometimes peer pressure can take us places we don't want to go: talking about people, cheating on tests, drinking, premarital sex, cursing, and more. Wanting be a part of the group is not a bad thing—until membership causes you to hurt others or yourself. If friends are forcing you to do something with which you don't feel comfortable, they really aren't your friends. All you can do is pray for them and continue to make sure that you follow Christ's example in your daily life.

APPLICATION

Today, examine the influence your friends have on you. List the positive influences, then the negative ones. Make it a point today to get rid of at least one of the negative influences.

PRAYER

Lord, thank you for the opportunities you have given me, and thank you for my friends. Bless me to seek those who will be a positive influence in my life and help me so that others see Jesus in me. Amen.

Day 3
BIRDS OF A FEATHER

Be ye not unequally yoked together with unbelievers.

2 CORINTHIANS 6:14

Nia needed to buy a present for Jessica's birthday. She agreed to meet some friends at the store that they said had some fantastic jewelry. As Nia headed to meet them, she saw in another store window a pair of earrings that she knew Jessica would love. She quickly purchased the earrings and put them in her purse. As she left, the door alarm rang. The clerk waved her through, however.

"Nia!" Amanda said when Nia reached the other store. "They have some really nice stuff in here."

Nia picked up a pair of gold earrings like the ones she had just purchased, but these were much more expensive. She quickly put them back. "How can you guys afford to shop here? Another store has the same jewelry for a lot less," Jessica said.

"Girl, we just take what we want. This store makes plenty of money. They're not going to miss a pair of earrings." Amanda said.
"Are you crazy? That's stealing," Nia said. "Thanks but no thanks." Nia headed for the door. As she stepped outside, the security alarm went off. She was shocked to see that the security guard was Deacon Smith from church.
"Nia Matthews, I can't believe you're stealing," he said after he took her to the office and discovered the earrings in her purse. He looked relieved when she handed him the receipt. "I'm glad. When I saw you with those girls, I was afraid you were up to no good."

Most of us have heard the saying, "Birds of a feather flock together." In most cases, you are drawn to your friends because you have things in common. Perhaps one of your friends likes to shop, which happens to be your passion. You may have skating in common with another. Just as you are often attracted to the positive things in others, you can be attracted to the negative. For example, we all know girls who are attracted to bad boys. Beware of the company you keep. You can have the best reputation in the world, but you will be judged as being a "bad girl" if you hang with the wrong crowd.

APPLICATION

Today during lunch, take a few minutes to examine the different groups at school. What are your impressions of them? Then, look at the group of people you hang with, and honestly ask yourself how others see you. If you feel that you are portrayed in a negative light, remove yourself from the group and find other friends.

PRAYER

Lord, please bless me to wisely choose my friends. Help me not to be so caught up in surface things that I forget to look at a person's heart. Bless me with the strength to find the right friends. In thy name, Amen.

Day 4
IT TAKES ONE TO KNOW ONE

And the Lord turned the captivity of Job, when he prayed for his friends:
also the LORD gave Job twice as much as he had before.

JOB 42:10

"Jess, do you consider me to be a good friend?" Nia asked during lunch one day.
"I think you're a great friend," Jessica replied. Why would you ask me that?
"I just wonder sometimes if I'm the kind of friend God wants me to be."
"What do you mean?" Jessica asked.
"Lately, I feel as though people are using me."
"People seek you out because you have a reputation for being a wonderful listener.
If there are times when you don't feel like listening, be honest with people. As far as
our friendship girl, I know you're here for me, and you know that I'm here for you,
and that's what's important."

Many of us do not give much thought to the kind of friend we are. You may take for
granted that you are a good friend, but are yo? Do you listen—I mean, really listen—
when others are talking or do you interrupt because you have to say what's going
on in your life? Do you make it a point to be there when your friends need you, or
do you offer excuses? Friendship is all about give and take.

APPLICATION

Today, hold yourself accountable, create a friendship meter. Make a list of all the qualities you desire in a friend, and then examine them to see if you live up to your own standards. If you don't know where to start, look at Corinthians 13, which offers the greatest definition of love, the basis of any friendship. Look at your list every now and then to see how you measure up.

PRAYER

Lord, from this day forward, bless me to be the best friend I am capable of being. Help me to be aware of the qualities of whether I am being used or am using others in the name of friendship. In thy darling son Jesus' name I pray. Amen.

Day 5
THE GREATEST LOVE OF ALL

He hath put my brethren far from me, and mine acquaintance
are verily estranged from me. My kinsfolk have failed,
and my familiar friends have forgotten me.

JOB 19:13,14

Jessica returned from Nia's house to find a letter from the University of Alabama lying on her bed. She took a deep breath and opened it. She had been accepted!

"Mom, Dad!" she yelled, running through the house. "I got in! I got into 'Bama!" She was met with empty silence. She quickly picked up the phone to call Jessica, but voice mail kicked in. She tried to instant message her but was unable to connect. *Why is it that when I have good news, no one is around?* Jessica thought.

You can share it with me, a small voice whispered. How could I forget to thank God? Jessica wondered. Without him, none of this would be possible. She quickly got on her knees and gave thanks.

Have you ever had a day when, no matter how much you want to talk to someone, no one is available? Your parents are unavailable. Your friends are not there for you. You may also have times when your heart is filled with sadness because of a bad grade, a failed relationship, or not getting the job you wanted. Turn to God. He is always there. When others turn their backs on you, he is there, still loving you and eager to hear you tell everything. God is the best friend any of us could have.

APPLICATION

Friendship pins—basically safety pins with beads threaded on them—have been a popular way to express that someone considered you a friend. Know that God loves you. Today, make your own form of friendship pin to remind yourself that Jesus is the best friend you could ever have.

PRAYER

God, thank you for being the ultimate friend and for being there for me during good times and bad, even though I am unworthy. Help me to follow your example. In Jesus' name, I pray. Amen.

WHAT GOD SAYS ABOUT LOVE
February

WEEK TWO: BOYS
Regina Gail Malloy

DAY 1 / The Nerd — Looks Aren't Everything

*Look not on his countenance or on the height of his stature;
because I have refused him: for the Lord seeth not as man seeth;
for man looketh on the outward appearance,
but the Lord looketh on the heart.*

1 SAMUEL 16:7

"Shaundra! Look who's on the cover of Black Enterprise magazine!" Cheryl exclaimed. "It's Jeremy Picolo! He's one of the richest young men under 30!"

"You mean old Pic'n' Pay from high school?" asked Shaundra. "He was such a nerd!"

"Well, honey, he ain't Pic' n' Pay no more. He's Pick and Paid! Cheryl said, laughing. "Remember, he's the guy who asked you to the prom, but you told him no because you thought Trey was sooo fine."

"Don't remind me!" Shaundra exclaimed. "Trey was so arrogant and rude. I don't know what I ever saw in him."

———

We all know at least one: the boy we call a "nerd." A nerd is someone who's usually very smart but not very popular or attractive. He may get straight A's in school, but if he's not cute, most of us wouldn't give him the time of day. Instead, the boys who are really fine looking are the ones who get the attention. However the Bible tells us that God doesn't look at people in the same way that we do. God is not concerned about how we look on the outside; he's concerned about our hearts and our thoughts. It's important for us to begin to see others as God sees them. When you're looking at a boy, find out what's in his heart. Whatever is in his heart will reveal who he really is (Proverbs 23:7).

APPLICATION

Think about one boy whom you find attractive. Write down three things that make him attractive. Then, based on Proverbs 23:7, write down three things about him that God would consider important. Now compare the two lists. If the lists don't match, begin looking at others the way God does.

PRAYER

Dear Lord, I'm so thankful you don't look at us in the same way that we look at ourselves. Lord, you see us for who we really are deep down inside. Lord, please help me to see others the way you see them. In Jesus' name, I pray. Amen.

Day 2
THE DOUGH, DOUGH
—I GOTS TO GET PAID!

But they that will be rich fall into temptation and a snare, and into many foolish and hurtful lusts, which drawn men in destruction and perdition.

1 TIMOTHY 6:9

Gregory, also known as "G-Rock," had more money than any other 17-year-old at school. He drove a BMW, wore the most expensive labels, and always carried a bankroll. It would be one thing if he worked hard at a job for the things he had, but that wasn't the case. G-Rock sold drugs for a living. Even though it was dangerous and illegal, he didn't care. The only thing that G-Rock cared about was "getting paid." Not only did he have a lot of money, G-Rock always had the prettiest girls. Several girls from school were always riding in his car or showing off some platinum jewelry that G-Rock had bought for them. They all thought he was "the man." It almost seemed like he was "the man" until he became the lead suspect in a multiple shooting.

Sometimes, boys will try to impress girls with the things they have. That's natural. Many times, girls are attracted to boys who have many material things. That, too, is natural. However, the key is making sure that neither one of you longs desperately to be rich. Having money and loving money are two different things. There's a big difference between someone with a desire to work hard at a legal job or to start a business, and someone who'll do anything for money.

APPLICATION

Think about a boy you know who may have a lot of money. Does he do something illegal or unethical to make his money? Read Timothy 6: 6-10. Think about where you think the boy will end up if he continues making money this way.

PRAYER

Dear Lord, I thank you for your Word. Lord, please help me to realize that anyone who loves money more than you is headed for a life of trouble. My desire is to keep you at the center of my life, knowing that you will give me everything I need. In Jesus' name, I pray. Amen.

Day 3
THE BOYFRIEND
—YOU SAY HE'S JUST A FRIEND?

A man that hath friends must shew himself friendly:
and there is a friend that sticketh closer than a brother.

PROVERBS 18:24

At fifteen, Tasha hung out only with boys. She said she didn't trust girls because they were always starting trouble. Tasha never dated the boys she hung with: she only saw them as friends. One day, Tasha met Darryl. She thought he was a great friend because she could talk to him about anything. Darryl, would tell Tasha about girls that he liked, and he even asked her opinion about whether he should date them. After a while, thought, Darryl started changing on Tasha. Instead of talking about others girls, he wanted talk about himself and Tasha. Then Darryl told her that he really liked her and wanted to date her. Tasha wasn't interested in Darryl that way. When she stopped hanging around him, Darryl started telling people that he had slept with her.

When Tasha heard this, she was devastated! Now everybody looked at Tasha as if she were "easy," and it was hard for her to defend herself because she hung around so many boys.

Boys may want to be friends with you for many different reasons, and sometimes the reasons are not the same as yours. Proverbs 18: 24 says, "There is a friend that sticketh closer than a brother." That's a great definition of a friend. That doesn't mean that you have to spend every minute of the day together. But it does mean that whatever your own brother would do for you, your real friend would do. If your male friend doesn't treat you the way a brother would, then chances are he may want to be something more than a friend.

APPLICATION

Make a list of all your male friends who say they want to be "just friends." Circle the ones who treat you the way Proverbs 18: 24 says a real friend should. Now check the names of those who are not circled. For each one, ask the Lord, "Why is this person in my life?"

PRAYER

Dear Lord, thank you for revealing to me how a real friend should treat me. Lord, I ask that you help me to select male and female friends who really care about me. Thank you, Lord, for being the best friend of all! In Jesus' name, I pray. Amen.

Day 4

PLAYA, PLAYA—HE LOVES ME, HE LOVES ME NOT

The lip of truth shall be established for ever:
but a lying tongue is but for a moment.

PROVERBS 12:19

Mario was one of the cutest boys that Rachel had ever seen. Every time Rachel saw him, he would stare at her and smile. One day during lunch, Mario came over and sat down next to her and they started talking. Rachel couldn't believe it! Within a week they started dating.

After two weeks of dating, Mario told Rachel that he was in love with her. Rachel didn't believe him until Mario gave her a diamond pendant with the words "Mario's True Love" inscribed on it.

A few days later, however, Rachel overheard two girls talking near her locker. "Girl, he even gave me this beautiful bracelet, and look what it says on the back: 'Mario's True Love.' Rachel knew they were talking about her Mario. Apparently he loved a lot of girls.

The words "I love you" may sound good, but if the person saying them doesn't really mean it, those words could be the most devastating ones you ever hear. A boy who says all of the "right" things without taking the time to get to know you is probably not serious at all. He's just playing. That's what a "player" does. He starts playing the game by choosing someone he thinks he can win over and then plays with her emotions, pretending that he cares just to see if she'll fall for it. Once she does, the player moves on to the next challenge.

APPLICATION

If there is a boy who's interested in you, write down at least three things that he's said to you about how he feels. Save the list and check it six months from now ago see if this behavior matches what he said.

PRAYER

Dear Heavenly Father, I thank you for being a God who cannot lie. Because you cannot lie, Lord, you have never hurt me with your words. Lord, I come to you today asking that you teach me how to know whether someone is telling me the truth. In Jesus' name, I pray. Amen.

Day 5

THE CHURCH BOY—SAINT TODAY, AIN'T TOMORROW

Be... an example... in word, in conversation, in charity,
in spirit, in flesh, in purity.

I TIMOTHY 4:12

Steven was very active in his church. He served on the Junior Usher Board and sang in the youth choir. He rarely missed Sunday service, and he was always the one selected to give the welcoming during Youth Day. The deacons and the mothers of the church said that they could see Steven becoming a preacher someday.

What the deacons and mothers did not know was that Steven was a different person when he was outside the church. In school, he was often rude to his teachers and would even curse them. Steven also had more than one girlfriend. He had his church girlfriend who sang in the choir with him, and he dated another girl who went to his school. There was even rumor that Steven got that girlfriend pregnant.

———

Anybody can carry a big Bible and regularly attend church services. However, the true mark of a Christian is behavior. It is important to look at the actions of a "church boy" and see if he really loves God or if he's just putting on an act. There are some boys who only go to church to socialize. In 1 Timothy 4:12, the writer shows us how we can tell if someone is truly a child of the Lord. The kind of person who is interested in serving the King is: an example to all that he teaches—in the way that he lives his life, in his love, in his faith, and in his purity.

APPLICATION

If you know any boys who say that they are Christians, think about how they behave outside the church. Does their behavior match the example given in 1 Timothy 4: 12? If not, pray and ask the Lord for guidance in your dealings with them.

PRAYER

Dear Lord, I thank you for showing me how a real Christian is supposed to act. Help me to better determine who really loves you and who doesn't. My desire is to know people who love you and want to be like you. In Jesus' name, I pray. Amen.

WHAT GOD SAYS ABOUT LOVE
February

WEEK THREE: ABSTINENCE
Yolanda Plunkett

Day 1 / Not Giving In—Mind Over Matter

Thou wilt keep him in perfect place,
whose mind is stayed on thee.

ISAIAH 26:3

Yvonne was fast approaching her senior year in high school. She had managed to get through all the peer pressure to smoke, drink, and have sex. Yvonne never had any interest in having sex, even though all her friends were doing it. But Yvonne knew in her heart that premarital sex is wrong. Yet one Saturday night, Yvonne met the guy of her dreams at a basketball game. Although she had a couple of boyfriends in the past, William made her feel unlike any of the others. He was gorgeous and treated her like a queen.

Yvonne and William dated for about six months and became closer than ever, but she noticed that he was starting to want more sexually than she was willing to give. Yvonne was in love with William and didn't want to lose him. She knew, however that she would have to make a decision that wold not go against her moral values.

The choice of remaining abstinent is a tough one. The media, movies, and music make it almost impossible to stay focused on purity. If you are confused and unsure, you can be pressured easily into going against your beliefs. Your mind must be stayed on God and his Word. It is right to say, "No, I'm not ready yet." Even better, say that you are saving your virginity for marriage. When you respect yourself and believe that you are the most precious person walking the earth, others will respect you as well. Losing someone because we choose to do what is right can be painful. When the pressure is on, turn to God, stay in prayer, and he will help you.

APPLICATION

Take one week and choose not to engage in any situation that may cause you to feel sexually tempted. If there is a song of a sexual nature on the radio, turn it off. Don't watch any music videos or television programs with sexual content. Say no to explicit conversations. Read inspirational books. Pray, asking God for strength and direction. After one week, acknowledge how refreshed you are. Give God the praise and keep it up!

PRAYER

Lord, you are the center of my joy and no one will come before you. Help me to remember that my body is a temple that is not meant for sexual immortality but for the Lord. Amen.

Day 2

PEER PRESSURE WHAT ABOUT YOUR FRIENDS?

It is better to trust in the Lord than to put confidence in man.

PSALM 118:8

Sierra was invited to the biggest party of the year. Lisa, one of the most popular seniors in high school, was having a birthday party. Sierra was excited to have been invited.

When they arrived at Lisa's house, the lights were dimmed low, the room was full of smoke, and there were no adults around. Sierra instantly felt uncomfortable.

When she tried to persuade her friends to leave, they said, "No way! We're having too much fun. Stop being such a square and go get one of the guys." Sierra knew that she had to leave—with or without her friends—and she knew that God was proud of her as she opened the door to walk out.

Peer pressure is one of the most stressful pressures there is. When our friends choose to do wrong, we must always pray for the strength to do right. The Bible states in 1 Corinthians 6: 18, "Flee fornication." Even if it means going against the crowd, we must be leaders and not followers. If we let God order our steps, we can expect great things.

APPLICATION

Today, let God use you to talk to your friends about all the great things that God has prepared for those who love him. Talk to them about your decision to remain abstinent and encourage them through Scripture to do the same.

PRAYER

Dear God, as others try to persuade me to do what is wrong, please guide me and give me strength as I try to do what is right. Be my friend when others turn on me, and hold my hand in any state of confusion. In Jesus' name, I pray. Amen.

Day 3
CONFIDENTIALITY
—WHOM DO I RUN TO?

In all thy ways acknowledge him, and he shall direct thy paths.

PROVERBS 3:6

Thomas's mother raised him in a very strict, religious home. His father had been killed in a car accident when he was three years old, and he did not have any brothers and sisters.

One day, Thomas and four of his closest friends were going to hang out at the mall, when one of his friends confided that he had gotten his girlfriend pregnant and he didn't know what to do. Thomas knew that a couple of his friends had experimented with sex, but he had not realized that it had become a regular practice. Thomas dated every now and then but had already made up his mind to remain a virgin until marriage.

When he got home later that day he felt uneasy about his friends situation. He needed someone to talk to and knew where he could turn. He closed his eyes to pray.

———

We should know that God's ears are always open to hear our faintest cry, and he'll answer each and every time we go to him in prayer. "Truly my soul waiteth upon God: from him cometh my salvation" (Psalms 62: 1). God will soothe our anxieties and calm our confusion, if we remember to cast our cares and worries upon him. Take it to the Lord in prayer.

APPLICATION

Today, find one person (mother, father, sister, brother, aunt, uncle, teacher, deacon, pastor, etc.) in your life that you feel you can talk to about anything. Sit down and talk, expressing your need to converse about any of life's concerns. Say that you want the conversations to be kept confidential, and ask if he or she feels comfortable with this arrangement. Always begin and end your conversations in prayer.

PRAYER

In the midst of my own worries and attempts to help others, God, please show me the right way. Thank you for watching over me in good times and in times of despair. Continue to guide me down the path of righteousness and give me the wisdom to show others the way. Amen.

Day 4
STANDING STRONG
—MISS GOODY GOODY

Fret not thyself because of evildoers, neither be thou envious against the workers of iniquity. For they shall soon be cut down like the grass, and wither as the green herb.

PSALM 37:1,2

Tracey and Beverly were best friends. They had known each other since birth and were now four months away from their high school graduation. The two young ladies were brought up in the church and had been active members since they could walk. As Tracey and Beverly entered high school , they were inseparable. They were on the honor roll, great at sports, and led their church in praise and worship on Youth Sunday.

Even though they both had boyfriends, they were virgins and planned to be so until marriage. Because Tracy and Beverly were doing so well in school and church, others began to envy them. They were labeled the "Miss Goody Goodies." Others tried to exclude them from senior activities and even started spreading rumors around the school, saying they were promiscuous .

When someone does or says something bad against us, it is almost second nature for us to want revenge. Or we may quickly try to defend ourselves, making a bigger mess of the situation. But the Bible states in Psalm 37: 8, 9, "Cease from anger and forsake wrath: fret not thyself in any wise to do evil. For evildoers shall be cut off: but those that wait upon the Lord, they shall inherit the Earth." When you take pride in yourself and your choice to remain abstinent, others will feel threatened and insecure. They may lash out, trying to bring you down. Lean on God during these times of slander. Continue to do good and good will prevail.

APPLICATION

Take some time and look through the Bible for all things relating to abstinence and sexuality. Print them on a piece of paper, cutting them into strips. Laminate the strips to make bookmarks. Give them to your friends at school or church who are trying to remain abstinent, for support and motivation.

PRAYER

Lord, help me to remember that the race is not given to the swift or to the strong but to the one who endures until the end. Hold my hand as I stumble; pick me up if I fall. Help me to be all that I can be, all that is pleasing in your eyes. Amen.

Day 5
EYES ON THE PRIZE

But be ye doers of the word, and not hearers only,
deceiving your own selves.

JAMES 1:22

At an early age, Troy had given his life to the Lord. He was now a junior in high school, kept good grades, was respectful to his elders, and attended church regularly. Troy was the guy that loved video games, girls, and the latest style of gym shoes. He wanted to go to college and become a doctor.

Troy had two older brothers who were both sexually active at a young age. One was in college and the other didn't do much of anything. His older brothers were nothing like him and teased him a lot about going to church all the time and about being a virgin. They told him that he needed to become a real man. But Troy had a different direction for his life.

———————

So many times, we know what is right but still choose to do what is wrong. When we keep our eyes on the prize of purity and continue to do things in God's way, we reap a harvest of blessing. Not giving in to our hormones or the negative advice of others can place us in a position of power—power over the negative, power to walk right, and power to talk right. God will provide us with peace and contentment in our hearts, and he will give us the wisdom to handle any situation that may block our path. "Delight thyself also in the Lord: and he shall give thee the desires of thine heart" (Psalm 37: 4).

APPLICATION

Today, start a journal about your journey of abstinence. Include the rough days and how you got through them. Include your good days, and be specific about how you continue to deal with the pressures of life and remain victorious. If you feel comfortable enough, share your journal with a peer who has a similar interest in abstinence. Praise God for your victory.

PRAYER

Father, today, I thank you for the grace and mercy that help me as I pursue purity. I pray that you will continue to watch over me as I strive to be my very best for you. Keep me humble, Lord. For it is not my will but thy will is to be done. Amen.

WHAT GOD SAYS ABOUT LOVE
February

Torian Colon

Day 1 / Jumping on the Bandwagon

For ye are brought with a price: therefore glorify God in your body, and in your spirit, which are God's.

1 CORINTHIANS 6:20

Eboni was feeling a lot of pressure about sex from her friends as well as from her boyfriend. Mason, her boyfriend of 18 months, was ready to take their relationship to the "next level."

"Look, Eboni" her friend Karla said, "Jason and I have been making love since we were 15 and we're almost 17 now, and I don't have any complaints. I know he loves me."

Eboni scoffed, "Jason breaks up with you a lot, he flirts with other girls in your face, and he says rude things to you. How can you say you have no complaints?"

"There you go again, being self-righteous." Karla lectured. "You better jump on the bandwagon, girl, so you can keep your man." Karla left and Eboni remembered her Sunday school teacher's verse from the previous week: "For ye are bought with a price: therefore glorify God in your body..." It was time to jump on God's bandwagon.

Are you a leader or a follower? Think about that. If you're a leader, then you will allow God's Word to work through you and get you through testing situations. In life, we are tested, but we can pass those tests if we follow God, not unbelievers. God wants his children to be readers and leaders of his Word.

APPLICATION

Make a list of friends that you could encourage to jump on God's bandwagon. Make it a point to express to them how important God is in your life. Your friends may try to encourage you to jump on their worldly bandwagon, but you have to stand firm on God's Word.

PRAYER

Lord, thank you for friends and relationships, but help me to stay focused on my relationship with you. I pray that my friends will see you in me and accept me for who I am. I only want to lean on you, my Lord. Amen.

Day 2
BOY, YOU FINE!

But because of the temptation to sexual immorality, each man should have his own wife and each woman her own husband.

I CORINTHIANS 7:2, (ESV)

Rhonda was in a sorority on her college campus, and she loved it. She also loved her fraternity brothers. Mainly B.J. One day during a party, Rhonda decided to get B.J. to notice her.

"B.J., you're looking nice in those jeans," she said, grabbing him around the waist. He turned to her with a surprised look.

"You're looking good in that skirt," he responded and checked her up and down. "How can I be down with you? I mean, I know you have a lot of women, but I..."

BJ slid his hand around Rhonda's waist. "Sweetheart, I didn't know you wanted to be down." Within minutes, B.J. had Rhonda on the dance floor, dancing to a slow song. He whispered in her ear, "Will you go home with me tonight?"

Immediately, Rhonda became nervous. What had she done? In that moment, she realized she wasn't ready for the next step-sex. Up to this point, she had abstained from sex, and she finally understood what her mother told her as she left to go to college, "There will be plenty of good-looking guys in college sweetie, but remember to save yourself for marriage."

It is important that young ladies understand that even if they start flirting with someone and then realize their actions have sent an unintended message it's okay to take a step back before things go too far.

APPLICATION

The Bible tells us that there is nothing shameful, dirty, or dishonorable about sex. In fact, God said that sex between a married man and woman is good and honorable (Hebrews 13:4). However, no one is perfect. If you are curious about sex (which is normal behavior), it is important to make a conscious effort to abstain from sex and focus on behaviors that are pleasing to God. And waiting until marriage to have sex is one area where God gives us specific instructions to wait until marriage.

PRAYER

Lord, guide me in the right direction. Lord, I realize that "going all the way" is not pleasing to You. Keep me focused on what your word says about sex so that I don't become involved in situations I may later regret. In Jesus' name, Amen.

Day 3
MAY I JUST HOLD YOUR HAND

*For the righteous Lord loveth righteousness; his countenance
doth behold the upright.*

PSALM 11:7

Travia dreaded her date with Devin because, although she was crazy about him, she was fed up with his hands. They were like the tentacles of an octopus. They were always all over her. Touching and feeling places they had no business touching and feeling. Devin's touch felt good to Travia's flesh, but her spirit kept telling her it was wrong.

Each time they had been together, Travia had become a little more curious about losing her virginity. She even went as far as going to her campus clinic to get birth control pills. But when the doctor began discussing her chances of getting pregnant, contracting sexually transmitted diseases, and experiencing the pills' side effects. Travia began to change her mind. After much prayer, she decided to be righteous, as God wanted her to be.

In order to have a good relationship with God, you have to weed out trouble. God knows what is best for you, and he knows your heart and mind. When your heart is broken, he is always there to hold your hand.

APPLICATION

Start a journal of decisions you've made and reflect on them on a weekly basis to see how each decision could have been different or more God-oriented.

PRAYER

God, please do not let go of me. Without your lead, I am lost. Keep me from straying into danger zones. Keep me from letting you go and grasping the hand of a person instead. Amen.

Day 4
STYLING FOR GOD

For all that is in the world, the lust of the flesh and the lust of the eyes,
and the pride of life, is not of the Father, but is of the world.

1 JOHN 2:16

Shelly was invited to a party with some friends. The young man hosing the function happened to be a guy at her high school on whom she had a crush.

"Make sure you dress really cute and sexy tonight," Shelly's friend Robyn suggested.
"But I don't have anything sexy."
"Well, you better find something if you want Kenny to notice you. I mean, you dress cute and all, but it's time you add a little more flavor to your wardrobe."

She searched her closet for something revealing that would make Kenny look at her. After all, her friends were wearing short skirts and shirts that exposed their backs. Finally, Shelly took her allowance and went to the mall. On her way into the mall, she saw Kenny. "Hey, Shelly Johnson, right?" he said in a very friendly tone.
"Yes"
"Hi, I'm Kenny Reed. I go to Jordan High. I've seen you around. I'm giving party tonight at my house. Would you like to come?
"Sure."
Kenny wrote down his phone number and address. "May I have your number, too?"
Shelly smiled. She had gotten Kenny's attention without following everyone else's advice. Being herself and dressing the way that God wanted worked just fine.

Think of times you have watched an awards show or other program where celebrities were present. One time a female artist stood on stage, wearing clothing revealing most of her body, and the first thing out of her mouth was, "I want to thank God..." When you looked at her outfit, it not seem as if she wanted to honor God above all.

APPLICATION

Do you want people to know you are a child of God? Take a look at your wardrobe and make two piles: one for the suggestive clothes and the other for the non-suggestive. If your non-suggestive clothes do not greatly outnumber the others, maybe it's time to get back in tune with God.

PRAYER

Lord, I want to represent you. I want people to see that I am serious about your undying love. Give me the strength to purchase clothes that represent my love for you and the things you stand for, not the things the world stands for. Amen.

Day 5
IF YOU LOVE ME, YOU WILL

*Blessed is the man that endureth temptation: for when he is tried,
he shall receive the crown of life, which the Lord hath promised
to them that love him.*

JAMES 1:12

It was prom night and Toya looked stunning in her deep purple, strapless gown. Her date and long-time boyfriend Tyrone, looked equally charming, and he couldn't wait to get Toya alone once he saw her. He had plans to cross their relationship over after the prom. Everybody in their class had gotten hotel rooms, and so had he. As soon as the limousine pulled away from Toya's house and she'd waved good-bye to her parents and friends, Tyrone started in about their big night.

"You look so good, baby," he whispered in her ear. "You know I have some condoms for tonight. Everything is taken care of."

Toya knew she had to tell Tyrone that she was not ready. *What will happen to our relationship?* she thought. Toya said a prayer and started to speak.

———————

"If you love me, you'll show me." "If you care, then you'll make love to me." Have you heard these lines before? Please understand that you are among thousands of girls hearing these lines. When you are propositioned with these statements, make sure that you retaliate with, "if you love me, then you'll understand why I want to wait for sex until I'm married.

APPLICATION

Take a moment to write down the pros and cons of beginning a sexual relationship. When you are finished, the cons will outweigh the pros. Remember, God is the one who knows how to truly love you.

PRAYER

Lord, I need to stay focused on you. Please enter into my heart, soul, and mind so that I can stay in tune with what you want me to do. Amen.

CONTRIBUTORS TO ORIGINAL W&G DEVOTIONAL PROJECT

Veronica Alexander	Jennifer Keitt
Eloise Averhart	Wanda Kimball
Kim Bailey	Ebony Lee
Nicole Bailey Williams	Portia Wills Lee
Sabrina Black	Regina Gail Malloy
Cynthia Brawner	Jacquelin McCord
Jazmyn Monet Childress	Trevy McDonald
Gwendolyn Phillps Coates	Jamell Meeks
Torian Colon	Janet Meeks
Anita Daniels	Stephanie Perry Moore
Adell Dickinson	Debra Nixon
Chandra Dixon	Yolanda Plunkett
Christina Dixon	Pam Rollins
Patrice Elliot Mace	Vanessa Salami
Tammy Garnes	Nicole Smith
Portia George	Marlow Talton
Jenise Gibson	Chandra Sparks Taylor
Rachelle Hollie Guillory	Edythe Thomas
Laverne Hall	Romana Tillman
Monique Headley	Raykell Tolson
Patricia Heggler	Marilyn Turner
Pamela Hudson	Karen Waddles
Francis Jefferson	Cherrill Wilson
Michele Clark Jenkins	Vickie Wilson
Winnie Clark Jenkins	Marsha Woodard

Today Is...

Goals for Today... ....
....
....
....
....
....
....

I will improve on this today... ....
....
....
....
....
....
....
....

I should have done this better yesterday... ....
....
....
....
....
....
....
....
....

I'm not going to worry about this today... ....

....

....

....

....

....

I'm praying harder for this today... ....

....

....

....

....

....

I give my Praise today by... ....

....

....

....

....

....

I'm reaching for... ....

....

....

....

....

....

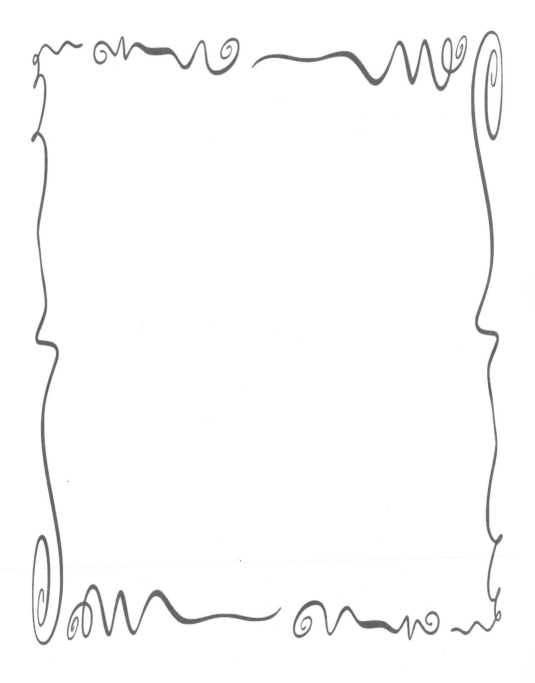

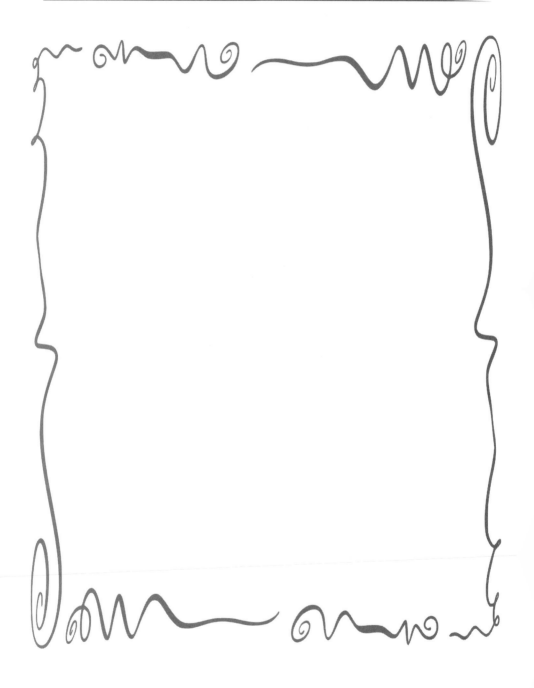

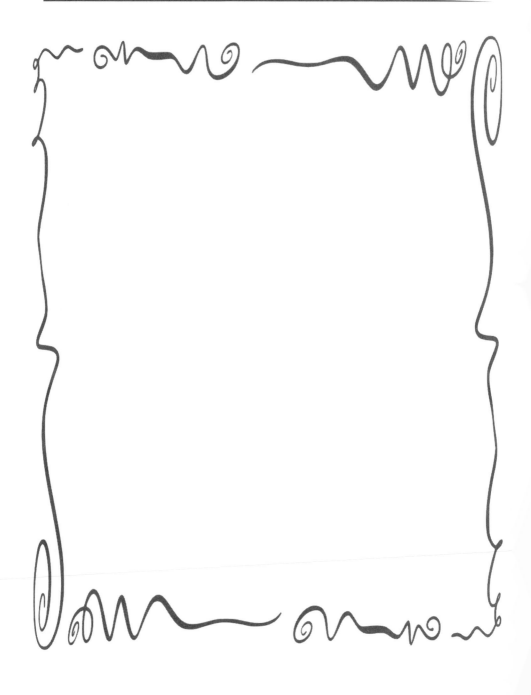

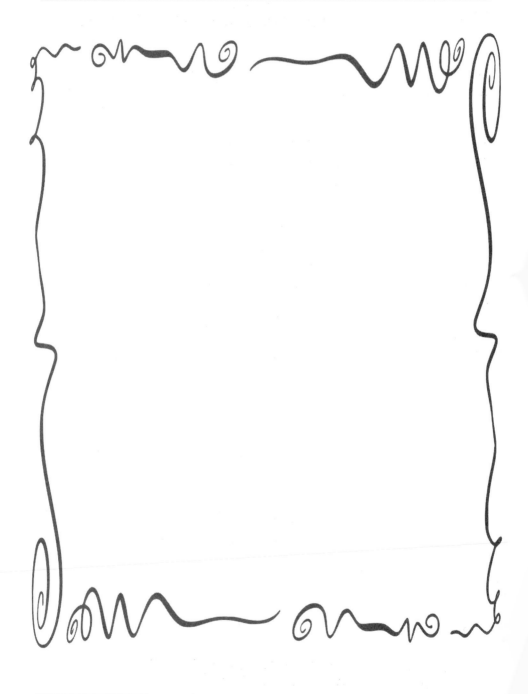

NOTES

223

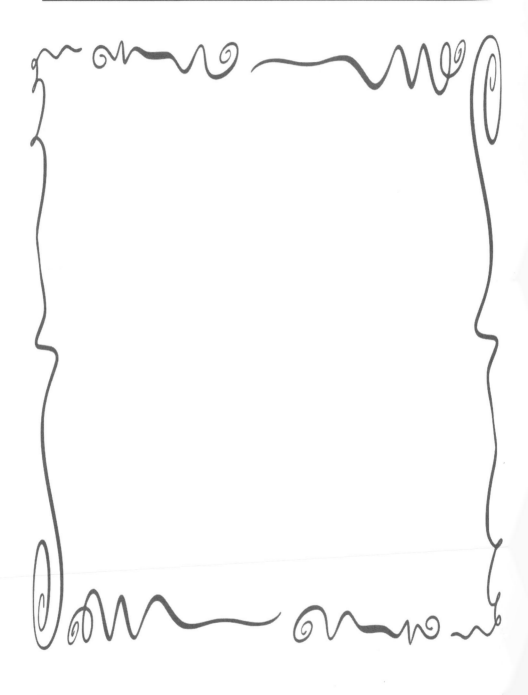